Malke Rosenfeld

Math ON THE Move

Engaging Students in Whole Body Learning

HEINEMANN
Portsmouth, NH

Heinemann
361 Hanover Street
Portsmouth, NH 03801–3912
www.heinemann.com
Offices and agents throughout the world

The author and publisher wish to thank those who have generously given permission to
reprint borrowed material:

Math in Your Feet™, LLC is a copyrighted and trademarked entity and the application
of this specific approach, as described and experienced in book form or during educator
workshops, is not for commercial use and is limited to individual educator classroom
implementation only.

Library of Congress Cataloging-in-Publication Data
Names: Rosenfeld, Malke.
Title: Math on the move : engaging students in whole body learning / Malke Rosenfeld.
Description: Portsmouth, NH: Heinemann, [2016] Includes biographical references
Identifiers: LCCN 2016037590 (print) | LCCN 2016041147 (ebook) |
ISBN 9780325074702
ISBN 9780325090146
Subjects: LCSH: Mathematics—Study and teaching (Elementary). | Games in
    mathematics education. | Movement education. | Dance in education.
Classification: LCC QA135.5 .R6845 (print) | LCC QA135.5 (ebook) | DDC
    372.7—dc23

LC record available at https://lccn.loc.gov/2016037590

Editor: Katherine Bryant
Production editor: Patty Adams
Typesetter: Gina Poirier Design
Cover: Suzanne Heiser
Interior design: Monica Ann Crigler
Manufacturing: Steve Bernier

Printed in the United States of America on acid-free paper
20 19 18 17 16 EBM 1 2 3 4 5

This book is dedicated to Dr. Patrick Hill (1939–2008), who oversaw two of my independent projects during my time at The Evergreen State College. His steadfast belief in my line of inquiry and his enthusiasm for my endless questioning about what it means to know, think, and learn in community have propelled me forward to this day.

Contents

Acknowledgments

I t is with great astonishment that I find myself writing these acknowledgments. In fact, it's unlikely there is anyone more surprised than me that I have actually succeeded in writing a book. The biggest thing I've learned in this process is that it takes a village to write one of these things, and so I have many wonderful, generous people to thank.

First off, thank you Jane Cooney for being a generous mentor and collaborator in the early years of Math in Your Feet, including hauling me to my first National Council of Teachers of Mathematics national conference! I am also indebted to Laura Friesen and Arts for Learning Indiana for taking my vision for Math in Your Feet seriously and for helping create strong connections with the Metropolitan School District of Pike Township in Indianapolis, where I was able to build and fine-tune the math-and-dance-making and learning experience. In particular, my thanks go to Dr. Sarena Shriver and Dr. Beth Niedemeyer for their support. I also want to thank all the fourth-grade students, teachers, and staff in the Pike elementary schools during the pilot years of 2004 to 2006. I worked with literally thousands of children during those two years and learned so much.

In the last five years I have been stupendously lucky to have fallen into a variety of unique and inspiring collaborations with some stellar math and arts education colleagues, all of which have led me to this book-writing project.

Nick Jaffe, your unwavering belief in my work and perspective has been a game changer for me. Thank you also for introducing me to Becca Barniskis and Barbara Hackett-Cox. Interacting with the three of you and your work around the *Teaching Artist Journal* and the Artist to Artist network literally transformed my understanding of what I do and why. Thank you all for asking smart, generative questions that always moved me forward. I am forever grateful for knowing and working with you.

Maria Droujkova, your big-picture mind and even bigger heart for both math and the people who do math have been, and continue to be, inspirations to me.

Christopher Danielson, running into you was the best thing to happen to my work and thinking in recent years. Your perspective on math learning is simultaneously grounded in the specifics and in the big picture, which has been immeasurably useful to me. Your mentorship and continued collegiality are what made this book literally possible. I can see evidence of our many conversations over the past few years woven into almost every chapter and I am sincerely grateful.

Max Ray-Riek, thank you for being you. Not only did you inspire me to start the book proposal process after Twitter Math Camp in 2014, but you are also a learner of the finest degree. I have so enjoyed the opportunity to think and learn with and from you.

I am indebted to Ilana Horn of Vanderbilt University for introducing me to Jasmine Ma of New York University as I endeavored to understand the general themes that make up the research on embodied cognition and how it might apply to the work I do in the classroom. Thank you to both of you, fine academics that you are, for your conversations, resources, and the willingness to make a personal connection between research and practice.

Although it's as decentralized as a professional learning community can get, I must absolutely thank the Math Twitter Blogosphere (#MTBoS) for being a crucial factor in my professional growth in the past few years. In particular, my conversations with the following fine folks, either in my Twitter feed, in their role as readers of draft chapters, and/or as mathematical inspirations of the finest kind, have all enriched my professional life. Huge, grateful thank-yous go out to Paula Beardell Krieg, John Golden, Simon Gregg, Suzanne Alejandre, Paul Salomon, Justin Lanier, Michael Pershan, Sue VanHattum, Andrew Gael, Kristin Gray, Tracy Johnston Zager, Chris Hunter, and Chris Robinson, among many, many others who inhabit that space.

Special and most grateful appreciation to two excellent educators: Jenn Kranenburg, whose story opens Chapter 3, and Lowell Miller, whose approach to extending Math in Your Feet to the page is detailed in Chapter 8. Thank you, Jenn, for your excellent intuitions about body- and moving-scale math pedagogy and for all the time and effort you put into telling me your story. And Lowell, I am hugely grateful for all our conversations about the learning you see happening with your students in the Math in Your Feet classroom.

I am also deeply grateful to my editor, Katherine Bryant, who took a chance on something different and was instrumental in helping me turn my ideas into something that I am thrilled to be able to share with others. Thank you, Katherine, for your patience as I learned how to write a book under your watch. I'm also appreciative to everyone at Heinemann who has helped make this book possible, especially Sherry Day, who has deftly handled the video portion of this book.

My appreciation also goes out to the following schools and educators, who allowed me to work with their students in preparation for this book:

- Many, many thanks to the Metropolitan School District of Washington Township in Indianapolis for allowing us to film students making math and dance at the same time. In particular, I am grateful for the welcoming, flexible, and friendly staff at John Strange Elementary School: Maravene Inmann, Kim Matsuoka, Kathy Brown, Jasmine Porter, Linda Dugger, Sonya Weber, Bert Goreki, and Maribeth Smith.

- Gratefulness abounds to the elementary teachers at Harmony School who have repeatedly opened their classrooms to my little experiments. Thank you, Lana Cruce, Matt Rosenthal, Jennifer Ruff, Laura Beth Wayne, and Claudio Buchwald, for all of your help with this project in particular.

- Thank you to River Birch Elementary School for your help and flexibility as I simultaneously worked with your students and collected video clips, photos, and conversations. I always love working with your students. I would especially like to thank Kris Kingery, Kristen DeHart, Bobby Coppage, Kristie Chalos, Jean Legge, Kristen Isbell, and Sarah O'Brien.

- Thanks to Michael Love and Cynthia Creek, of Rogers Elementary School and Rise Reinier, and Kevin Gallagher, of Templeton Elementary School, and the Monroe County Community School Corporation, for allowing me to work with your lovely and inventive primary students.

To Ana Maria, lots of love and appreciation for all of our conversations over tea and walks around the park during the book writing. Thank you also for the metaphor about the difference between knowing how to cook mac and cheese from a box and learning to cook four-course meals. It didn't make the final edits but was nonetheless a lovely sentiment about the learning process. Learning takes time.

And last, but definitely not least, my family. I have been instructed by my daughter, Isobel "Izland" Casey, to thank her for the "tenacity" she has exhibited during this long season of book writing. I figure she's been patient with me and all of my late nights, so it's the least I can do to fulfill this request. I believe my husband, Mike Casey, has also exhibited a positive and tenacious attitude, and I love the both of you to pieces. Thanks especially for your support during the last couple of crazy months of this journey.

Foreword

Maybe you are standing at a conference, or library, or your computer reading this foreword as you decide whether you're going to read this book. I would strongly suggest that on your way home with the book, or added to your online shopping cart, you pick up a roll of painter's tape.

This is a book that deserves to be not only read, but experienced. As I read, I taped out a square and a grid on the floor, and stepped and slid and jumped my way through this book, and my understanding of mathematics and student learning is richer for it.

During the process of writing the foreword for this book, I got the chance to join Malke Rosenfeld as a fellow learner in a mathematics workshop about tiling and symmetry. We were both challenged by the task of using only paper and pencil and visualization to imagine what different sets of five square tiles (pentominoes) would look like if they were rotated, reflected, and translated.

Inspired by what I had learned from *Math on the Move*, I began to wonder: would this task be different if we changed the scale from paper-size to floor-size? Like the students who participated in the "Scaling Up" (p. 42) and "Collaborative Rope Polygons" (p. 55) activities, would we have new insights (and new challenges) if we explored the shapes by taping them out on the floor, or trying to use our bodies to make them?

I also wondered what it would feel like to be embodying the shape, instead of looking at it. I thought of how in all of the Math in Your Feet lessons, there's a period where students are in the observer role, and a period when they are in the maker or doer role. How might my experience of these tiling shapes be different as a doer rather than observer?

So we went out into the hallway, taped down a grid, and instead of visualizing and drawing, we figured out how to step the paths of our pentominos. I wasn't sure what would happen if we made these changes, but we were richly rewarded. Suddenly, not only did the shapes make more sense, but it became easier to transfer our learning back to paper and pencil as well! We made sense of the pentominoes, got better at drawing them, and learned new ways to think about reflection (changing every "left" to a "right" and vice versa in our paths made the reflection of our pentominoes) and rotation (rotating our bodies before we made the path made a rotation of our pentominoes). We generated new questions to explore and had new insights into our original questions!

This experience turned me into an evangelist for *Math on the Move*. I encourage you to spend some quality time reading and rereading Chapter 3, in which Malke lays out a "zero-entry pool" for getting your feet wet with body-scale moving mathematics. What I love about that chapter is that the experiences she describes, like making figures bigger than a sheet of paper, or experiencing lines and grids that are big enough to walk around on, can become a regular habit when students are struggling with any concept related to space and/or patterning. I now routinely ask myself, "How might students think about this differently if they were in it, walking around, rather than outside it, drawing it on paper?" That question never would have occurred to me as a mathematical thinking question without *Math on the Move*.

I feel a need to confess, before we get any further, that I thought of myself, before reading this book and getting a chance to dance with Malke, as someone who is clumsy and better at cerebral pursuits like math than embodied pursuits like dancing. Through reading and dancing I came to two big realizations.

First of all, I realized than in *Math on the Move*, the math is the dance and the dance is the math. Dancing is not just a trick to help me remember a math idea that I could access another way. Dancing the same as my partner *is* congruence. Dancing in the opposite way from my partner *is* reflection. For students who are great athletes or dancers but don't see themselves as great mathematicians, letting moving math come into the classroom gives them a chance to be the math experts. Are they the best at spotting or describing congruence in shapes they look at? Maybe not. But they can be the best in moving congruently with their partners.

Second, I realized that my fear of dancing was analogous to many peoples' fear of mathematics. I had never given myself permission to take dancing risks, make mistakes, and learn! The warm inviting tone of the book, and my experiences getting to work in person with Malke, helped me enter into a mental space where I could test out new dance ideas, and if I made mistakes at first, keep working until I got better . . . or change my ideas and try something I could master.

Whether you are a confident mover who is still learning how to bring that joy to your mathematical explorations, or a confident mathematician still learning how to be fluent in your precise movements, or someone for whom dance and math both sound intimidating, I think this book will inspire you to try something new. Malke shares stories of students learning about how to work in a group, how to have calm control over their bodies and their ideas in order to make new, creative inventions, and how to use mathematical and movement creativity to find joy in thinking, making, mapping, explaining, and sharing.

I would encourage every reader to pick up some tape, make some lines, grids, or shapes on the floor, find some kids, and get moving. Keep these questions in mind:

- How does being inside this body-scale space give me new insights and questions?
- How am I taking risks, trying new things, making mistakes, and learning?
- How am I supporting others to help them take risks and learn?

You'll find a new joy and creativity, and rigor and precision, in your moving and math that will help you see the world in unexpected ways!

Introduction

> Most people feel that they have no "personal" involvement with mathematics, yet as children they constructed it for themselves. Jean Piaget's work … teaches us that from the first days of life a child is engaged in an enterprise of extracting mathematical knowledge from the intersection of body with environment. The point is that, whether we intend it or not, the teaching of mathematics, as it is traditionally done in our schools, is a process by which we ask the child to forget the natural experience of mathematics in order to learn a new set of rules.
>
> —Seymour Papert, *Mindstorms*, 206–7

I am quite aware, when describing the work I have done since 2004 to help children make math and dance at the same time, that the Math in Your Feet program is the perfect blend of the two most anxiety-inducing disciplines for most of us raised in American society (and I'm only half joking). For one thing, both math and dance have a lot in common in their apparent ability to invoke fright and a flight response. They also share the deep-seated myth that we as a culture hold about learning and knowledge: that you are either good at math or dance or you're not. I think this is partly a case of self-fulfilling prophecy but more likely a result of how both subjects have historically been taught in a "Here's how you do it; now do it on your own" kind of approach.

Despite these deep-seated cultural attitudes, I know from experience it is possible to move beyond the fears related to both math and movement. In school I was always a happy geometry student but never numerically literate. Until recently, my numeracy was about on par with every other American's; that is to say, every time numbers came up in conversation, I'd get this funny tight feeling in my chest and change the subject. So, it was a little alarming to me when, after developing the Math in Your Feet program, which at the time focused mostly on geometry topics, I began to realize there might be more math in the dancing the children were creating—and that not only did I not know what it was, but I had no idea how to start figuring it out. It was an uncomfortable feeling, but one that I ultimately could no longer ignore, spurring me into an ongoing inquiry into what it means to "do" mathematics, and specifically what it means to learn and make math.

Although I used to think that math was some kind of inaccessible, abstract magic trick, a sort of in-joke that excluded us common folk, these days I appreciate that math is not that at all. The reality of math as most of us know it is like that story where three men are standing in a dark room touching different parts of an elephant. None of them has the full picture because each one perceives only isolated, individual elements of the whole animal. The reality, I'm discovering, is that math is just like that elephant: a large, expansive, multidimensional, intelligent, sensitive, expressive creature. The problem is that most of us have been standing around in that dark room since about kindergarten, grasping only its tail and thinking, *This is what math is and, personally, I don't think it's for me.* We've been unable to see the larger, incredibly beautiful picture that would emerge if only we would turn on the lights. Or, in reality, if we could find someone who would help us understand what we are looking at once those lights go on. I aspire to communicate this larger picture of math as engaging, beautiful, and personally relevant in all my teaching work.

But my work is not just about the math. As a visiting teaching artist, I provide children experiences with percussive dance (styles like tap dance, step dance, and clogging) in both performance and workshop settings. In workshops and longer-term school residencies, my goal is to provide students with enough of a feel for the art form and its basic movement vocabulary and skills so that they can quickly begin to experience the core of the discipline—the process of making their own foot-based dance patterns. I do this in the way I structure the learning space and the learning and making processes themselves. Every activity, student demonstration, and emergent skill builds on the one before it to illustrate the following tenets:

We can create completely original ideas using the language of rhythm and patterns in our feet.

There is a process to making something new.

We can be musical, mathematical, and physically expressive at the same time.

Little ideas as expressed through the rhythm and pattern we make with our feet can go together to make bigger ideas.

We can relish and celebrate the effort it takes to do this.

In this book I illustrate and explain how children can become both dance makers and math makers at the same time and, more generally, what makes math and movement such effective partners.

A Different Approach to Learning

It is the partnership itself that influences and defines the learning that happens at the intersection of math and dance. Sometimes this intersection is called *arts integration*, but in my experience this is a somewhat inaccurate term. To me, the word *integration* implies that there is some kind of merging between the arts content and the other discipline, when, in reality, efforts in this direction are often like a sixth-grade dance: yes, the boys and girls are all in the same room, but they stick to their own sides of that space, and never the twain shall meet. Arts integration is challenging to do in a meaningful way, no matter what subjects are being brought together. In her post "STEAM-Roller" on the *Education Week* blog *Teacher in a Strange Land*, Nancy Flanagan (2013) wrote: "I like a snappy multiplication-facts rap as much as the next guy, but the fact is—it's not easy to integrate rich arts practice or content into science and math instruction. Especially when the assumption is that good curriculum begins with 'core subjects,' the arts acting as a kind of color commentary." When paired with math learning, the whole moving, dancing body definitely needs to be more than color commentary or a wallflower at that sixth-grade dance.

These days I prefer to call what I have done to bring math and percussive dance together simply *interdisciplinary learning* because that is the most accurate description. Both math and dance are discrete disciplines that require students to gain content knowledge, develop skills, and cultivate thinking and reasoning fluency in order to create meaning within their respective systems. However, as I illustrate throughout this book, the process of bringing math and a moving body together, whether within the system of dance or at *moving scale* (which is explained and illustrated in more detail in Chapter 1 and Chapter 3) is not as straightforward as one might think. First of all, we need to take a close look at our current practices of how we engage children's bodies in the classroom. Too often the moving body is used primarily as an object for literal interpretation, illustration, and memorization of math concepts. Conceptualizing the body in this way, as a drawing or mnemonic tool, severely limits its potential in a learning setting.

Deborah Ball has said that math pedagogy "must be based on the structures of the discipline in order to avoid corrupting or distorting its content" (1990, 4). This statement rings true for the discipline of dance as well and, most important, has implications for how we conceptualize, create, and execute interdisciplinary curricula. We can't make up the dance to fit the math, nor can we make up the math to fit the dance. This book is, in part, about how we can harness our students' inherent *body knowledge* (a term coined by Seymour Papert, 1993) to help them develop new understanding and facility with mathematical ideas that often seem remote and impenetrable to our learners.

This new body-based understanding can be developed and supported through a making process. I see some parallels between arts-based learning and the maker movement and maker education; in both settings the focus is on the design and construction of objects in response to a perceived need, which allow for high learner agency, experiential learning, and a chance to tinker—to play around with a set of ideas until you land on an answer that makes sense to you, creating your own understanding and meaning in the process. The results of math-and-dance making, however, are a little more temporal, a little less tangible, and they require us to look more closely for evidence of learners' growth during the process. Regardless of the product developed, both the maker movement and I have been highly inspired by Papert's work and thinking about design environments in which kids learn the language of mathematics in the context of *using* math to make something new. There is meaning in the making, and by that I mean the making of tangible things and also the making of a larger understanding about how ideas work, how they are connected to other ideas, and how these ideas become useful objects with which to create a place for ourselves in the world. In my view, the territory of learning needs to include experiences where learners get really messy, dig in, try things out, make mistakes, and arrive at multiple right answers as well as learning in more formal contexts. It's the real-life experiences that are essential for children as they work hard to learn how to communicate their own and others' ideas.

Why We Should Use the Body in Math Learning

In this book I endeavor to explain why we should use the whole, moving body in math learning by pulling from both research and practice to build a framework for meaningful, body-based math learning, but the short answer is that when children harness their innate body knowledge for mathematical sense making, they also harness their whole selves in the pursuit of new ideas and understanding. They develop, communicate, and reason about mathematical ideas both nonverbally and verbally. Teachers regularly report to me during the math-and-dance work I do with their students that they cannot believe how much the children are "talking math" while they endeavor to meet the physical and mathematical challenges presented to them and during other parts of the day. To me this makes perfect sense because this is how we learn the meaning of words in the first place—in context. Children can make good sense of the world when they get a chance to interact with it, and children are also well able to reason with and about things they observe and do. But they can do this only if they get the chance to do, make, investigate, converse, wonder, build, express, and reflect. Without these kinds of interactions they might still be able to memorize math facts, but memorization would not necessarily mean they would know, for themselves, that something was true.

About This Book

In this book I focus on what it means and looks like to bring meaningful movement and math learning together in the classroom. It is completely understandable if you initially have reluctance, doubts, or questions about using movement in math class. This reluctance could be, in part, related to the fact that lots of us have really learned math only as it's presented *on* the page or as a series of rules, facts, and procedures to memorize. Math learning using the whole body can feel and look very different than what we're used to thinking of as math. But experiencing math this way can become a potent opportunity to create new insights about the math ideas not necessarily or immediately accessible to us as represented visually on the page. We want math to make sense to our students, and the moving body is a wonderful partner toward that goal. Of course, trying out any new approach for the first time may induce a little trepidation, but this book (and its online video companion) is filled with everything you need to get started: the whats, the whys, and the hows of helping learners make math meaningful through purposeful, whole-body-based math investigations and problem solving.

What's in the Book?

Chapter 1: The Body as an "Object to Think With"

In this chapter I provide an overview of what meaningful whole-body math learning looks like in my own and others' math and dance classrooms. I also provide a conceptual framework and pedagogical base for teachers wishing to engage their students' whole bodies in mathematical sense making.

To access Math on the Move's *online resources:*

Go to www.heinemann.com and click the link in the upper right to **Log In.** (If you do not already have an account with Heinemann you will need to **Create an Account**.)

Register your product by entering the Code: MATHONMOVE.

Once you have registered your product, it will appear in the list of **My Online Resources.**

Chapter 2: How Is This Math?

I provide the answer to the common question "How is this math?" through illustration and description of the kinds of mathematics that can be explored, learned, and expressed by the moving body, including spatial reasoning, dynamic geometry, part-whole relationships, equivalence relations, and mathematical thinking and sense making.

Chapter 3: Beyond Mnemonics: Getting Started with Moving-Scale Math

This chapter provides a number of options for getting started with non-dance, whole-body, moving-scale math learning in your classroom. It also functions much like a zero-entry pool in that you can get your feet wet by adding students' whole bodies into the math you are already doing and then, as you build experience and confidence in this new mode of teaching and learning, venture in a little deeper.

Chapters 4 and 5: Implementing Math in Your Feet

In Chapter 4 I detail the first three stages (understand, experiment, and create) of the Math in Your Feet lesson progression for grades 3 through 6, which can also be adjusted for second graders in the second half of the school year. In Chapter 5 I lay out the final three stages of math-and-dance making (combine, transform, and communicate).

Chapter 6: Facilitating the Math-and-Dance Classroom

In this chapter I lay out the three main strategies for facilitating a moving, math-and-dance-making classroom. I also discuss considerations for learners with special needs.

Chapter 7: Adapting Math in Your Feet to the Primary Grades

The work primary students do in Math in Your Feet looks similar to the work intermediate students do, but the pace and tone of that work are necessarily different. In this chapter I provide a lesson progression specifically tailored to this age group and highlight how the process of creating maps of their math-and-dance patterns is integrally intertwined with the math-and-dance making itself.

Chapter 8: Assess, Extend, and Connect

How do you assess the work and learning of moving students? This assessment is tied to the ways in which you help students extend and connect their moving math learning in the form of mapmaking, written reflections, and word studies. In this chapter I detail what this looks like and also provide suggestions for where and how to connect the moving math to other, more familiar math-learning contexts.

Math on the Move's online resources

To access *Math on the Move*'s online resources go to **www.heinemann.com** and click the link in the upper right to **Log In.** (If you do not already have an account with Heinemann you will need to Create an Account.)

Register your product by entering the **Code: MATHONMOVE.**

Once you have registered your product, it will appear in the list of **My Online Resources**.

Chapter One

The Body as "An Object to Think With"

As teachers we know kids love to move—in fact, there's a developmental imperative at play that cannot be ignored. But how can we harness this innate and essential playfulness in our students in a way that moves them, literally, toward conceptual understanding of elementary mathematics? Using the moving body in math class is about more than getting kids out of their seats to get the wiggles out or to memorize math facts. Instead, we need to treat the movement as a partner in the learning process, not a break from it.

Meaningful Connections Between Math and Dance

When I first wondered if there might be math in the dance making I had been doing with elementary students, I knew I didn't know enough math (yet!) to pair the two in a meaningful way and that I needed an interpreter to help me connect the two. I was very lucky to be introduced to elementary math specialist Jane Cooney, who became a generous resource and mentor. In my first meeting with Jane I described how I dance on my small square dance board (more traditionally called a *step-a-tune*) and the many ways that I supported children in becoming dance makers using the elements of percussive dance. Neither Jane nor I wanted to make up the math to fit the dance or to change the nature of my traditional dance form to fit the math. Considering this balance between the math and the movement is possibly the most important issue to attend to when bringing movement of any kind into math learning. The challenge lies in navigating the palpable tension between the physical, kinetic existence of the body in time and space and the often static nature of mathematical concepts we encounter on the page. At the beginning of my journey, I had experienced math only as fixed and as a series of facts already decided, composed primarily of two-dimensional images and immutable right answers. But I also suspected that some of those math ideas could be explored in the percussive dance making I did with kids. So Jane and I set about looking for useful connections between the two disciplines. After some experimentation during my two pilot years of working with fourth and fifth graders in a large school district in Indianapolis, Indiana, I established five themes around which all our work revolves:

- *Patterns:* Students create, observe, descre, and compare patterns; the creation aspect has similarities to a language arts writing-and-revision cycle.

- *Problem Solving:* Students solve problems with a focus on mathematical thinking and sense making and relevant math practices.

- *Combination:* Students engage in a highly interesting mathematical activity that also ups the physical thinking and problem-solving challenges for students.

- *Transformation:* Students work as a team to reflect the original math-and-dance pattern over a line of reflection.

- *Communication:* Students speak about and reflect fluently on their ideas and the decisions they've made in the process, in both math and dance, through written, spoken, body-based, rhythmic, and symbolic language.

Each theme represents and makes explicit a shared idea found in both math and dance and points to the ways we use the math to build and describe our dance patterns to the mutual benefit of both subject areas.

My biggest takeaway when thinking about bringing the math and percussive dance together was that both dance and math are discrete disciplines; both are meaning-making systems in their own right with their own aesthetics, traditions, content, and pedagogy. It's really not reasonable to expect that there will be a one-to-one correspondence between every idea in both disciplines. There are, however, places where the two overlap in gorgeous ways, and this book is full of what I've discovered at the intersection of percussive dance, mathematics, and learning; how we can translate these insights to nondance movement; and how you can bring that into your own classroom. Still, as I continue my inquiry into this topic I am continually reminded that *not all of dance is mathematical and not all math is danceable*;

in particular, the moving body is not always the most useful tool for expressing and representing every mathematical idea. (I'll dig more deeply into the math itself in the next chapter.)

Criteria for Meaningful Moving-Scale Math Learning

My own search for meaningful connections between math and percussive dance started with a question; the answers I've found since then also have relevance for learning math at moving scale (also called walking-scale or body-scale), outside a dance setting. These phrases indicate that the scale of the learning activity now allows enough room to freely use the whole moving body in a mathematical investigation. To create a meaningful context in which children can think deeply and engage in mathematical sense making with their whole bodies, the following elements must be present. I'll discuss these in more depth in the rest of this chapter and in the chapters that follow.

- *The math-and-movement lesson provides a structure in which students make choices, converse, collaborate, and reflect verbally on what they did, how they did it, and what they noticed while they were engaged in whole-body-based activity.*

- *The body activity is focused on mathematical sense making, not mnemonics, often through efforts to solve a physical or moving-scale challenge of some kind, not on illustrating a math idea as it is typically represented on the page.* The most appropriate mathematics for whole-body investigations are, as described in the next chapter, found on the action side of math, something the moving body is perfectly situated to express and explore.

- *The teacher is the facilitator of the activity, pacing, and discussion.* The teacher's role in this learning-while-moving approach is not about instruction or acting as the ultimate expert. Instead, the teacher is more of a facilitator, supporting learners and their collaborative relationships as they work toward addressing and reflecting on the challenge in question and, later, connecting the mathematics as represented and experienced in the moving challenge to new modes or contexts. The teacher questions, makes observations, and moderates discussions, all of which help children understand both the math ideas and the activity in which they're engaged from multiple perspectives.

● *The activity explores one or more mathematical ideas at a new scale.* Typically, math investigations in K–6 classrooms happen at hand scale or paper-and-pencil scale, meaning through the manipulation of hand-sized objects or within the confines of a piece of standard notebook paper. Creating a math task at moving scale means you can be engaged in one of two different but related approaches. The first approach is making a familiar math object, like a hundred chart, bigger so that it is big enough for a whole body (or bodies) to explore. The second approach involves focusing on the scale of the *activity*. When a student stands up to move her whole body to interact mathematically with her peers and the environment, she will experience and notice different aspects of the math ideas under investigation.

● *Students experience the activity as both doers and observers.* We can create new perspectives and new meaning when we are literally at the center of the action. We also need a chance to observe the action from outside of the experience; observing others work and/or listening and watching as they explain their reasoning has the potential to give us insights into our own work, exposing things we might not notice while we are engaged in the activity.

● *In partnership with the change of scale, the math-and-movement activity should be explicitly connected with the same math idea as it is experienced in other contexts, scales, or modes.* Providing multiple opportunities and modes in which to investigate a particular mathematical idea helps students become more flexible problem solvers and better understand how the idea can be used and applied in different contexts. This means, in part, that during or after a moving activity there should be an opportunity for verbal or written reflection on the experience (both the activity and the math); a chance to gather and analyze data created by the movement challenge; or time to create a map or a more formal record of the activity.

Bringing Meaningful Movement into Math Learning

How can we engage the moving body in a way that is pedagogically sound and useful for both disciplines (not to mention beneficial for our students)? Here are three dance-based examples that exemplify a positive balance between the math and movement and reflect the previous criteria.

Kindergarten: The Quality of Numbers One Through Five

With the guidance of a teacher, a class of kindergarten students have created a dance using the numbers one through five and are onstage, performing for their families. Although we think of numbers as something to count, the children are not counting out the beats to the music or counting the numbers while they dance. Instead, the children embody the quality of each number, starting with one child at a time crossing the stage. As the dance begins there is energetic Irish fiddle music playing and, as the teacher calls out, "One!" individual students begin to cross the stage with scarves waving, moving and dancing as the music moves them. Some walk forward, others backward; some skip, some jump, and some turn as they go. It's clear they've had a chance to explore ways to move through space including a variety of locomotor movements and are able to make their own in-the-moment choices for this dance. After all the students have crossed, the teacher calls out "Two!" and the whole class returns to the stage, each looking around for a partner with whom to dance. When they find someone to dance with they face each other, which makes each grouping of two clear to both the students themselves and their audience. When the teacher calls out, "Three!" the students must hold scarves in a ring of three and then turn in a circle. When they hear, "Four!" they make groups by putting their hands on the shoulders of the kid in front of them and walk around the stage as four-person units. They end their dance with "Five!" by creating five-person frozen sculptures (Ruggery 2012).

The dance has a clear sequence and is developmentally appropriate for the age group. By this I mean that the dancing has not been overly prescribed and is not reliant on technical skills beyond the ability of this age group; the work is also obviously personally relevant to the individual children. In terms of the math, the children express their understanding of the numerical groupings by actually putting themselves in the groups with no prompting from the teacher. Their dancing also illustrates how we can use movement to express dynamic mathematical ideas, in this case the real meaning behind the numerals 1 through 5, and emerging understanding of groups, which is an important core concept for multiplicative thinking later on down the line. Most importantly, the children are operating in a moving and changing system within the dancing itself and are able, with little prompting, to navigate their way through both the math and the movement. In a sense, it's hard to tell the difference between the math and the dance. Being able to do both at the same time is what brings the excitement and meaning of ideas expressed through both disciplines to the stage.

Second Grade: Contrasts

Teaching artist Kimberli Boyd has second-grade students start a math-and-movement lesson by creating a body shape while standing in place and then finding a contrasting shape. For example, if one shape means stretching tall, the contrasting shape would be something that is close to the ground. They continue the lesson by performing contrasting motions (fast and slow, smooth and sharp). A child demonstrates a movement that Kimberli describes as "controlled and kind of slow"; then Kimberli asks the class, "What is the opposite motion?" The class replies, "Fast." In another contrast, children are now in pairs; one partner is still while the moving partner travels around him or her. To close the lesson, Kimberli has groups demonstrate what they've learned during the activity; the class watches as two groups of students demonstrate tall and short, fast and slow, smooth and sharp, moving and still and, finally, "one final shape to end the dance" (DetroitYouthVideos 2013).

In this lesson (which is appropriate for first and third graders as well), the language of dance is expressed verbally and through the movements of the body; the language and movement together provide fertile ground for exploring the mathematical ideas of logical opposites and difference. It's also a great way to support kids in exploring new ways to move their bodies. By blending basic movement concepts of what the body can do in time and space (move or be still, grow or shrink, perform sharp or smooth movements, and so on) with the idea of *contrast*, students have the opportunity to engage personally and viscerally in understanding the ideas of difference and opposites.

Fifth Grade: Symmetry

A class of fifth graders is exploring the dynamic ideas embedded in reflection symmetry. The teacher reviews reflection symmetry visually in two-dimensional space on an overhead projector before the students review how reflection can be created using three-dimensional body shapes and movements. The teacher asks the fifth graders to find words to describe why they think another student has created a symmetrical shape with his or her body and then engages the whole class in brainstorming revisions to make the pose more symmetrical. These are key skills needed for analysis in both math and dance modes; in particular, using specific language and identifying properties in the context of dance making make students' dances stronger and more interesting. The lesson progresses from individuals demonstrating symmetry in their own bodies to teams of students reflecting their partners' movements, as different groups bend, twist, and turn their bodies. One student illustrates what it means to put children literally at the center of their own learning when she says: "When you do math worksheets you usually do it for a teacher for homework, but when you dance it you're doing it for yourself" (Caspersz n.d.).

In all three of these moving-scale and math-and-dance activities, what stands out the most to me is the equal time and attention paid to both the math and the dance, that the body is not relegated to the role of illustration, that learners have agency over their moving bodies in a way that they wouldn't in a teacher-created, student-memorized dance, and that neither the math nor the dance is singled out as the sole reason for the activity. In a moving-scale approach the goal is the same: the activity is both the mode and the context in which students work to access the mathematics.

Avoiding Limited Uses of Movement in Math Class

While the classroom vignettes in the previous section illustrate useful examples of what meaningful math and movement can look like from the outside, we also need to consider nonexamples. What does *less meaningful* math and movement look like? There is an image that gets forwarded to me every six months or so by people who know I am interested in both math and dance. The original picture and its variations are titled "Beautiful Dance Moves" or "Function Calisthenics" or something related. In the picture a stick figure poses its arms in various graph shapes, with the graph's equation written below each figure. Although this picture, which gets passed around so often, must feel meaningful to many people, re-representing the original two-dimensional representations of graphs with your body to memorize them is not what I would consider mathematical sense making.

Here are some other examples of classroom activities I've seen that illustrate using the body as a tool for learning math in limited ways. Despite these limitations, most of the following activities are helpful for some aspects of learning math; there are times when we need multiple strategies for memorizing our multiplication tables so we can engage more freely with other math ideas and challenges. However, from the standpoint of *combining* math and a whole, thinking, expressive, moving body, especially if it's within a dance system, I find these activities narrowly conceived—not just in the math and the dance but in the learner's role as well:

- using arms to create symbols for operations, like $+$, $-$, and $=$ (focusing on creating representations of the symbols, not expressing their meaning)
- using hand movements in a song about memorizing a procedure

- putting arms into the static shape of lines, graphs, or angles as they are represented on the page

- jumping on the beat in a predetermined pattern while skip counting

- bouncing on an exercise ball while reciting multiplication facts

- singing a song with an accompanying dance about finding the area of a circle, using movements that bear no relationship to the properties of a circle

- exploring a math concept such as high versus low in isolation, removed from a narrative context (such as retelling a story) or the larger context of dance learning and making

- having multiple students become the sides of a triangle by lying on the floor

The issue for me lies not only in the fact that each of these examples treats math as simply a set of rules and facts to be learned but also in the fact that the teacher has provided specific instructions for movement and physical patterning in each activity. Even if the math-learning goal stayed the same (memorizing facts or procedures, for example), most of these activities would become immediately more meaningful if the children had a role in developing the movement choreography. Starting with the question "How can we think about or show this math *idea* with our bodies?" and offering multiple opportunities for children to contribute their own ideas and build something new as a group creates a more significant experience for the learners.

The Body as a Thinking Tool

The three more meaningful activities described on pages 5–7 are strong examples of purposeful movement in math class. They also exemplify what Seymour Papert, in the preface to his seminal book *Mindstorms* (1993), identified as *body knowledge*. In these examples, the learners' existing body knowledge is both harnessed and deepened in an environment that provides thoughtful, math-informed, movement-activity sequences facilitated by the teacher.

The Power of Body Knowledge

The phrase *body knowledge* is such a potent one. It is a challenge to our collective conception of what knowledge is and where it resides; it also places the student in the very center of the learning process. Body knowledge, also referred to as *embodied cognition*, helps us understand the processes of thinking and learning with our bodies. This is something we begin developing from birth. Developmental psychologists have shown that in babies, "cognition is literally acquired from the outside in" (Smith and Gasser 2005, 13). This means that the way babies physically interact with their surroundings "enables the developing system [the baby!] to educate [herself]—without defined external tasks or teachers—just by perceiving and acting in the world" (13). Ultimately, "starting as a baby [as we all did] grounded in a physical, social, and linguistic world is crucial to the development of the flexible and inventive intelligence that characterizes humankind" (13).

Understanding what embodied cognition is and what embodied learning looks like is the focus of a multidisciplinary group of cognitive scientists, psychologists, gesture researchers, artificial intelligence scientists, and math education researchers, all of whom are working to develop a picture of how we learn and think with our bodies. Some of these researchers are focused more specifically on a variety of ways the body is involved in learning and expressing mathematical ideas. Much of their focus has been concentrated on the way our hands express ideas in concert with speech; this kind of research has shown clearly that gestural expression plays a large role in thinking through and expressing mathematical ideas (Alibali and Nathan 2012). Gesture research has become a strong platform on which to develop even more insights into a thinking, moving body. From here, other researchers have concentrated on the use and benefits of hand-scale tools and manipulatives; still others are focusing on the whole body as the primary actor in embodied mathematical activity (Hall, Ma, and Nemirovsky 2015)—quite literally as the "object to think with" (another enduring phrase coined by Seymour Papert) within a mathematical investigation. In general, the research over the past few decades has resulted in a general acceptance that it is impossible to ignore the body's role in the creation of mind and thought, going so far as to agree that that there would likely be no mind or thinking or memory without the reality of our human form living in and interacting with the world around us.

Sense Making with the Body

Since the publication of *Mindstorms*, the phrase *body knowledge* has often been used to describe what is happening in situations where children are primarily using their hands or eyes (often in front of computer screens) or in *any* situation in which a child is out of her seat and moving. The fact is we all use our bodies to interact in, through, and with the world, all the time, every day. Given the inevitability of our bodies being present in some way in everyday learning, the questions then become *What does it mean to use and develop body knowledge?* and *How can we incorporate or harness this idea in the pursuit of rich conceptual understanding of mathematics?* My ongoing concern has been about the common assumption that body knowledge is created or used simply by moving a part of the body or being on one's feet. This is what is assumed when, for example, a student is shown how to make a static representation of a right angle using her arms. This activity is unnecessary because this piece of math can be explored and identified in many different contexts and is already quite familiar to upper-elementary students if they've had a chance to explore it on the page. If you follow up with a question about the measurement of a right angle, kids will be able to tell you that answer, too, because it is a math fact they have memorized, often without struggle. The real potential for using the moving body in this situation is investigating questions like these:

What are angles, really?

What do they do?

What is the relationship between a right angle and other kinds of angles?

What might happen if we combine two or more right angles?

These questions are interesting in and of themselves and also because they instigate some interesting new thinking and question asking, as well as new opportunities for application. Investigating what angles really are is also a question that a moving body is perfectly primed to explore. An angle is an amount from *here* to *there*; ninety degrees is the result of a rotation from *here* to *there*; and the moving body is the perfect tool for exploring *here* to *there*.

While we can *see* children's bodies moving, it is not always an easy or intuitive process to understand the mathematical learning happening and the knowledge expressed while their bodies are in motion. The challenge lies in navigating the palpable tension between the physical, kinetic existence of the body in time and space and the often static nature of mathematical concepts we encounter on the page. However, while it might appear that the images of mathematical ideas are frozen on a page in time and space, much of math is, as I detail in Chapter 2, actually about action, movement, and relationships.

In a sense, the moving body is best conceived as a tool for *thinking through* or making sense of a mathematical question to find an answer or create new insights not accessible through conventional means. From the very beginning of the Math in Your Feet work, we present children with the challenge of creating their own dance steps while simultaneously using math ideas to inform and describe what they are doing and why. They respond by thinking through this challenge with their bodies in a way that is at once dance, physical thinking, and mathematical problem solving and sense making. This kind of activity is similar to how math manipulatives or other thinking tools can be used in math class. Considering the role of hand-based manipulatives in math class can help us create a conceptual frame around the work we might want to do with whole, moving bodies in mathematical investigations.

The Purpose of Thinking Tools in Math Class

Math manipulatives include, among many others, pattern blocks, snap cubes, Dienes (base ten) blocks, and counters. They have the potential to help make the sometimes elusive ideas of quantity, pattern, transformation, and structure more visible to learners. Most often used in K–2 classrooms, their potential does not stop there; physical models and other handheld objects are useful at all levels of math learning. In my own recent experience I explored symmetry groups by turning and flipping a paper square and triangle in various sequences with my hands, writing down my results, and looking for patterns in the table I created. It was the movement inherent in this activity that strengthened my understanding of the rotations and reflections and their relationship to each other in a way I could have not done through internal visualization alone. The action involved in *moving* (flipping, turning, sliding, building, constructing, drawing) while working through mathematical inquiry and problem solving is, I believe, one of the most important aspects of using math manipulatives and other handheld tools in math class.

What does it mean that students are thinking through math ideas while using these kinds of hand-scale tools? The answer to this question can inform our efforts to put the moving body to good use in pursuit of a strong conceptual understanding of mathematics. Master math educator Henri Picciotto (n.d.) makes clear that tools are generally used in two ways: either prescriptively or as an opportunity for guided exploration:

> Tools can be used poorly, and often are. Manipulatives can be "taught" in a "this is how you do it, now practice" style that works so poorly with so many students. Electronic tools are often used in a "do this, do that, what do you notice?" style which suffers from the misconception that students will notice the thing we want them to notice.

Intelligent lesson design using learning tools is often based on a reversal of traditional teaching practice, and the creation of "no threshold, no ceiling" problems. . . . The problems need to be engaging and accessible, but at the same time they should be worthy of reflection, collaboration, and discussion.

A thinking tool in math class, then, is not the object itself but the context in which it is used; it is a context that requires learners to engage with the materials, the math ideas, and classmates to create mathematical meaning, whether they are investigating number patterns or geometric attributes or making sense of information in a problem-solving context. Other distinguishing factors of objects as thinking tools include high learner agency, a chance to learn through dialogue with peers, and an understanding that there might be multiple paths to the end goal even if, ultimately, everyone gets to the same answer.

As an example, let's think about pattern blocks, a collection of wooden or plastic shapes (equilateral triangles, two different rhombi, hexagons, squares, and trapezoids) that are used to create geometric designs and patterns and offer the opportunity for exploring symmetry and noticing relationships between the shapes. Pattern blocks can be used in many ways, often through guided inquiry, both geometric and numerical. Elementary teacher Simon Gregg gives his third- and fourth-grade students the challenge of coming up with multiple versions of a dodecagon using pattern blocks; you can also challenge students to see how many different hexagons they can make using the same materials. Both scenarios are examples of identifying a learning goal and allowing for learner agency and exploration within the task itself. Chris Hunter is a math coach who has used pattern blocks in a different but still guided approach, this time focused on numbers, geometry, and algebraic thinking. He asks his students to engage with questions like these:

- *You have 6 hexagons and 4 trapezoids. What is the greatest and least perimeter you can make?*
- *How many ways can you find to show me $\frac{1}{2}$? Can you describe it another way?*
- (When given an increasing pattern) *How many in figure 100? Figure* n?

If you can create this kind of structure around mathematical exploration with handheld objects, you can also do this with the moving body in the classroom.

The Body as a Thinking Tool

What do we want the mover to do and to learn? This is a critical question for anyone set on using physical objects (including the body) in math learning. Just because a child has an object in hand (or is up out of his seat) does not mean he is learning math. It is not the object itself that supports the student in coming to know and understand but rather the context in which that tool is used. Deborah Ball has also written about the importance of creating context when using manipulatives. "Although kinesthetic experience can enhance perception and thinking," she writes, "understanding does not travel through the fingertips and up the arm. And children also clearly learn from many other sources—even highly verbal and abstract, imaginary contexts. Although concrete materials can offer students contexts and tools for making sense of the content, mathematical ideas really do not reside in cardboard and plastic materials" (1992, 47).

Put another way, using tangible, moveable objects (including the moving body) can be useful in math learning as long as attention is paid to the math *ideas* as well as what you do with the object. Being on your feet is not a guarantee of either developing or using body knowledge in mathematics—and it goes the other way, too. Just because you're a skilled mover does not necessarily guarantee you will be good at math. The meaning is created through thoughtful construction of activities or even whole sequences of investigations where each mode, mathematical and movement, comes to influence the understanding of the other.

Here is another useful excerpt from Deborah Ball on the topic of manipulatives, but this is also where my analogy between a moving body and inanimate objects used in math class diverges. The moving, learning body is more than an object—it is the whole child interacting in and with the larger environment (classroom culture, peers, teachers, and the physical space in which the activity is occurring.) So, where Ball uses the words *manipulative* and *material*, I have substituted *body* and ask you to instead imagine the animated, curious children who populate your classroom:

> Unfortunately, creating effective vehicles for learning mathematics requires more than just a catalog of promising [bodies]. The context in which any [body] . . . is used is as important as the [body] itself. By context, I mean the ways in which students work with the [body], toward what purposes, with what kinds of talk and interaction. The creation of a shared learning context is a joint enterprise between teacher and students and evolves during the course of instruction.

Try It Yourself! Part 1

Before you go further, get a roll of masking tape or painter's tape. Measure out four equal lengths of tape, each two feet long. Use the individual pieces of tape to make a square on the floor.

Start with your feet together in the center of your square. How many ways can you think of to split your feet apart (using a jump to get there)? **Hint:** You can rotate your body to face different directions in your square. Does that give you some new options?

Developing this broader context is a crucial part of working with any [body]. (1992, 18)

This passage perfectly describes the dynamic of teaching and learning in Math in Your Feet and at moving scale.

What "Thinking Through" Looks Like with the Whole Body

The moving body is truly a multidimensional object to think with and needs to be treated as such—a true partner in learning. What does it look like to think through a math idea while dancing or, indeed, to think through making a dance step using math ideas? Here is an example within Math in Your Feet, where children are thinking through a math-and-dance challenge with their whole bodies.

Thinking Through "Not Quite the Same"

Fairly soon after students start making their first four-beat dance pattern (pattern A), I introduce the idea of *sameness*, as in "How can you dance the same as your teammate?" or "How can you and your partner dance the same as each other?" When dancers do the same moves at the same time, this kind of sameness is called unison. Here, two boys are working together, using their bodies and conversation to clarify some issues that are keeping them from dancing in exactly the same way. These boys have facility with the dancing but are still working to understand and clarify the direction of one specific turn in their pattern. In the following exchange, my role is one of observer as they work to clarify sameness in their dancing.

> **Me:** [Watching them dance together and noticing some differences in the last two beats] *OK, let's do it beat-by-beat, OK?*
>
> [The boys dance one beat at a time, at a slower tempo, counting together.]
>
> **Me:** [Talking to Juan] *So, you know what I noticed? I noticed you were turning your body a little differently in that corner. Let's try again. Look at each other's feet and see what happens.*
>
> [They do the dance again. Their last two beats are still different from each other.]
>
> **Me:** *And also, on those last two beats, I noticed you're turning right and you're turning left. So why don't you work on . . .*

Juan: [Quickly gesturing left with his right hand] *We'll turn left.*

[The boys dance but turn on the second beat instead of the fourth.]

Me: *Try one more time? One, two, three . . . no, no! It was on the fourth beat you were turning.*

Boys: *Ohhh!*

[Juan gestures and demonstrates to Dalton turning right with his body; then they dance.]

Me: *Oh, hold on!* [Talking and gesturing to Dalton] *You need to go that way. You're turning right on the first one and then a right turn again. Aha! There you go, that's it. So try that again. . . . One, two, three. . . . Yay, that's great!*

In the actual experience the boys' movements were more intense and kinetic than I've transcribed it here. I appear to be talking a lot in this segment, but every time I noticed something that was not the same, the boys immediately started moving again to figure out how to correct it. Their bodies did the thinking; my role was to observe their work and provide some outside perspective about and language for the relevant properties that were not yet being danced the same. In math, the idea of sameness can also include discussions and analyses of differences, similarities, and change and we need shared language and awareness to do this. Being physically involved in trying to *make* sameness and difference moves the conversation from the more familiar activity of identification to a brand-new experience of literally embodying the concept.

Thinking through specific challenges like sameness and difference (illustrated in detail in other parts of this book) while engaged in making dance and math at the same time is a collaboration between the body and all its senses (Hall and Nemirovsky 2011), the influence of one's partner or collaborator, the kinetic energy distributed around the room as everyone works, and the words we use to talk to ourselves and communicate as precisely as possible to others. Thinking through mathematical and movement ideas at the same time positions the body as a dynamic object to think with and allows learners the opportunity to think deeply about core mathematical ideas in new and novel ways, which I explore in much more depth in the next chapter.

Try It Yourself! Part 2

The boys in the example were clarifying the direction of the turn on the fourth beat of their pattern. Here is a turn challenge of your own to try!

Put your **feet together** and **stand** in the center of your square dance space. **Turn** your body right, toward the first side. **Turn (while jumping)** toward the next side. **Turn** toward the third side. **Turn** toward the fourth side. How many times did you have to **turn** to get all the way around? How much, in fractions, did you **jump** on each turn? If you turned one-fourth of the way around each time you jumped, how much was each rotation in degrees?

If you **jump** and **turn** halfway around your square, how much have you rotated? How many jumps will you need to get all the way around? If you start your movements facing forward, **jump** and **turn** ninety degrees to the right and then **jump** and **turn** 180 degrees to the left, where will you end up?

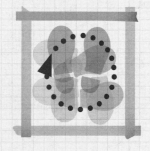

Chapter Two

How Is This Math?

Because math is frequently presented in a static way in textbooks and on worksheets, the dynamic action and meaning represented by those symbols and figures are often lost in the shuffle. The experience of math as a series of fixed images, ideas, and answers might leave us to wonder: *How on earth can we actually learn math if it's not written down?*

What Are the Nouns and Verbs of Math?

When we think of math, what often comes to mind are the nouns, the mathematical *objects and procedures* that can be named or identified visually. In truth, mathematics is a balance between objects (the nouns) and actions (the verbs). The body is best positioned to express the action side of math, not only in the thinking that happens while doing and learning math, but also in the expression of mathematical concepts that are in and of themselves action oriented. The interwoven relationship between the nouns and verbs of math comes to light when I brainstorm with educators about what kinds of math we might find in dance making. A list of representative educator responses can be found in Figure 2.1.

Although it might appear as if I've set up an either-or situation, the nouns and verbs of math are actually in what Anna Sfard calls a "complementary" relationship, meaning that they are two sides of the same coin (1991, 4). You can't have one without the other. For example, it is impossible to have a full understanding of symmetry as reproduced in static form on the page.

Brainstorm: What kind of math can you find in dance?	
Nouns (objects)	**Verbs (actions)**
Patterns (units, cycles)	Transform
Geometric forms (line, angles, shapes)	Rotate
Fractions (part-whole relationships)	Reflect
Symmetry	*Patterning*
Direction	*Unitizing*
Spatial reasoning	*Compose/decompose units*
Multiplication (groups)	*Sequence*
Properties	*Combine*
Rate/time	*Compare*
Constraint	
Formation	
Set/group theory	

▶ **Figure 2.1** The list on the left always fills up first; the one on the right often has markedly fewer initial entries. The italicized words in the right-hand column are ideas I usually have to add after we have identified the relationship between the two lists.

The action of *transformation* is an integral part of conceptualizing and generalizing the concept as a whole. Understanding the nature of an angle is another example. Students must synthesize the relationship between three individual but related conceptions: an angle as a static geometric form, as a measure, and as a rotation. The rotation in itself can be hard to conceptualize because that movement is either depicted as a static figure (imagine curved dotted lines between one ray and the other) or enacted by turning an object with no visual clues for the starting or ending position, making it hard to determine the distance or measure of the turn. In a more general sense, mathematics is an activity in which to be engaged as much as subject matter to be learned. The verbs on the action side of math are about the *things we do* and *how we think* as we are working mathematically to solve a problem and build a rich conceptual understanding of the discipline at the same time.

What Mathematics Can the Body Best Learn and Express?

You might well be asking yourself, *How is this math?* or, more to the point perhaps, *How is this learning math?* Throughout this chapter I answer this question by describing and illustrating the kinds of mathematics topics and practices that can be explored, learned, and expressed by the whole, moving body. The categories include the following:

- *spatial reasoning and orientation*, including experiences of and reasoning about location, distance, direction, and magnitude, all of which support numeracy and mathematical reasoning across topics
- *dynamic geometry*, including constructions, angles, and rotations
- *part-whole relationships* (composing and decomposing shapes and numbers)
- *equivalence relations*, that is, the math of making comparisons while evaluating sameness, similarity, difference, and change, including transformations and symmetry
- *mathematical thinking* and sense making

Every point on this list can be experienced, explored, and learned in some capacity through the whole, moving body.

Spatial Thinking and Reasoning: The Foundation of Mathematical Understanding

Spatial thinking itself is a nonverbal mode of knowing and reasoning originating in the body. It includes the ability to know where you are in space and decide how you will move yourself or objects through that space. Strong spatial thinking skills, in general, have been shown to "vitally inform our ability to investigate and solve problems, especially non-routine or novel problems, in mathematics" (Sarama and Clements 2009, 161). Spatial reasoning has been shown to transfer between mathematical topics. In short, developing and using spatial thinking and reasoning is a key aspect of what helps us understand and make sense of math. Although popular conceptions of spatial skills point to an ability to manipulate and rotate two- and three-dimensional shapes in the mind's eye, spatial reasoning skills are far more diverse than this. In fact, studies emphasize "the importance of self-produced movement [not just visualizations] for success in spatial tasks and suggest the benefit of maximizing such experience for all young children" (Sarama and Clements 2009, 188). The free online document *Paying Attention to Spatial Reasoning*, published by the Ontario Ministry of Education (Queen's Printer for Ontario 2014), provides a comprehensive list of the many ways spatial reasoning can be expressed and developed. The following are examples of tasks in which we can involve the body in spatial reasoning and orientation:

- moving one's whole body in or through space
- creating or designing objects (in Math in Your Feet, this means dance-based pattern units)
- navigating or way finding
- composing (units, shapes, or numbers)
- using nonverbal reasoning
- locating objects and remembering locations of objects
- orienting
- diagramming

When we combine these physical actions with the intentional use of language, especially location, distance, orientation, direction, and geometric vocabulary of rotations, translations, and transformations, we have the potential to create a strong learning environment not only for the development of spatial reasoning in our students but for their mathematical success as well (Queen's Printer for Ontario 2014).

Spatial Reasoning and the Moving, Learning Body

Math education researchers Julie Sarama and Douglas Clements define spatial sense as "all the abilities we use in 'making our way' in the spatial sphere" (2009, 198). When you bring the moving body into math learning, you create a huge opportunity for conversations about and experiences with moving in and through space. Although we are born with innate ability for spatial thinking and exploring space with our bodies, it is clear that explicit encouragement and practice is needed to develop spatial reasoning skills and have an effect on math learning. Without a formal place in the curriculum, it can be challenging to figure out how and where to fit experiences with spatial reasoning into an already busy learning day. The National Research Council has stated that "spatial thinking is not an add-on to an already crowded school curriculum, but rather a missing link across that curriculum. Integration and infusion of spatial thinking can help to achieve existing curricular objectives" (Committee on Support for Thinking Spatially 2006, 232). Happily, a whole-body approach to learning math can provide a rich, meaningful context in which to integrate conscious and creative exploration of space while covering math topics and building conceptual understanding of math at the same time.

Spatial Orientation and Navigation

Where are you? Where do you want to go? How are you going to get there? These are the core questions of spatial orientation. When working within a dance system, and the inventory of movement and spatial vocabulary that implies, we are required to become more conscious about how we move through physical space. This creates really fun and interesting challenges for our students as they build a new a set of movement skills while reasoning themselves from one place to another.

In the Math in Your Feet classroom, we start our math-and-dance making by finding our *center*. This word refers to both the dancer's center—a place of balance from which we gain control and move outward—and a literal center in the middle of a two-by-two-foot taped square that acts as a frame to define the dancing space. Next, we orient ourselves to the directions in which we can move. At first, while we are focusing solely on directions (point to the front of your square, now point to the right side, and so on), this new space seems straightforward and perhaps even simplistic. The complexity soon increases as we start to add in other variables, such as how to move ourselves from one place in the square to another (jump, slide, step, turn, and so on) and the positions our feet can take (split apart, crossed, left or right foot) when we land in our intended spot.

Precisely executed foot-based patterns are the result of knowing where you are and thinking ahead to where you want to be, both of which require the dancer to have a clear sense of direction and purpose. One small change to the classroom floor with a bit of blue tape creates a formal space and a creative constraint in which to clarify where one is and the directions in which one can move. With this frame, kids are better able to talk with their partners about where they are and where they want to go while they make their patterns. With the sides and corners of the space clearly marked, we know where the center is, the front, the back, the right and left sides, and our diagonals. We can navigate this territory even when we've changed which way we're facing. The more we move in and around this space, the more oriented we become spatially and mathematically.

Making Dance Maps

Moving through space and representing that movement are two separate but related competencies. Spatial concepts (often in concert with geometry) underlie many numeric concepts. Number lines, array structures, coordinate grids, visual representations of fractions, and models of volume using cube blocks are all examples of how spatial concepts and geometry support numerical understanding. Mapmaking itself is a mathematical activity that generalizes the specifics of physical space and represents them in schematic and symbolic form; mapmaking is also the flip side of moving through space. In elementary school, representing lived experience in map form using (initially) invented notation is an authentic way to develop geometric and spatial reasoning while also attending to specific geometric concepts. It is also a valuable way to help students move toward conceptual understanding of ideas represented by more formal graphing notation in the fifth and sixth grades.

Learning to move between representational settings is a key part of mathematics. When students map their dances, they are changing their representation from physical to symbolic. This process abstracts the context from physical to graphic and requires learners to decide which details in the dance context they want to communicate and how that might look in visual or schematic form. The maps in Figures 2.2, 2.3, and 2.4 represent primary students' understanding of position, location, and direction and serve as a record of their experience with creating a four-beat dance pattern within a square dance space. They also illustrate the diversity of

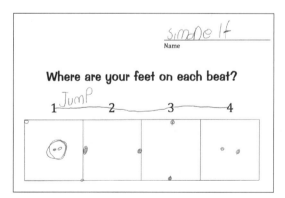

▶ **Figure 2.2** Notice the word *jump* and a line connecting all four beats: on every beat, you jump to the new position.

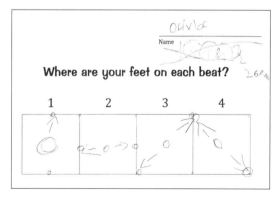

▶ **Figure 2.3** It's always really exciting to see how many different ways kids represent their dance patterns to great effect. This second grader used arrows to indicate the direction of the movement.

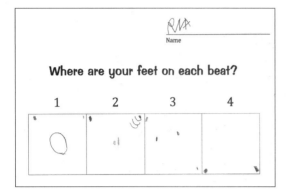

▶ **Figure 2.4** The kindergarten girl who created this map was very precise about where her feet were in the square. On beat 1 the dot represents a *step* in the front left corner of her dance space. The exciting thing here is that she figured out a way on beat 2 to be very clear about the fact that the left foot stays put and the right foot moves into place (notice the little waves in the upper right corner of that box).

what younger kids are capable of. This was their fourth math-and-dance session with me and the second time they had seen this reflection prompt. Up to this point I had only modeled a very basic notation system to record the location of the feet in the square, including a circle in the middle of the square to remind them of their starting position. The prompt was purposefully fairly open and related to the dance pattern they had made that day with their partners: *Where are your feet on each beat?* This assignment was about assessing direction and location only. The kids themselves initiated the extra information they thought they needed to communicate their dance patterns, such as identifying the movements (steps or jumps) that got them where they wanted to go.

Dynamic Geometry: Angles and Rotations

Spatial orientation and geometric thinking are closely linked. Geometry ideas "underlie all mathematical thought . . . from number lines to arrays [spatial representations], even quantitative, numerical, and arithmetical ideas [all] rest on a geometric base" (Sarama and Clements 2009, 200). Rather than a set of rules and procedures, geometric reasoning is "the ability to make reasoned judgments regarding relationships and properties, and describe, define, justify, and generalize geometric ideas" (234). The geometry topics most easily recognized and most fully explored in the Math in Your Feet work are angles and rotations. These topics also carry a multitude of misconceptions in both teaching and learning. Although it's sometimes treated as obvious in elementary math classrooms, developing a useful understanding of angle has been shown in both research (Smith, King, and Hoyte 2014) and practice to be extremely challenging for learners but critical to students' success in high school math courses like trigonometry. Conceptualizing angles actually requires a learner to experience and apply understanding of a number of different ideas simultaneously. The child must develop an understanding that an angle can be conceived as three separate ideas: a part of a geometric figure, a measure, and (often the most difficult idea to understand) a rotation.

Fortunately, exploring these ideas dynamically using both hand-based manipulatives and the body helps develop this understanding. For example, when using the whole body to execute a rotation through space, it is pretty much impossible to track or measure how far you've turned without some kind of visual reference, so the constraint of the square dance space comes in handy. When you've decided on a starting place, you orient yourself to your front (the direction you're facing before you start moving). From there you can turn to the first, second, or third side—a 90-degree, 180-degree, or 270-degree turn, respectively; additionally, sometimes children will start turned 45 degrees, which adds a layer of challenge. Being able to visually track the starting location all the way through to the ending position provides a visceral, proprioceptive (meaning a sense of one's own body in space) experience for children, which results in a new ability to talk about their own turns and identify the measurements of the turns that others have included in their math-and-dance patterns.

Example: Reasoning About Rotations with Bodies and Language

The whole class has just finished warm-ups. I've introduced a number of turn combinations during this time over the last few days, including 90- and 180-degree turns (but not both in the same combination). Today we've danced a 90-degree turn to the right followed by a 180-degree turn to the left (so we've ended up facing our left side). I've paused our activity to see what the kids think about this new situation.

> **Me:** *Tell me what we did in that pattern. How far did we turn on those two turns?* [Three students offer different ideas: we turned "a 180," we turned "a 90," and we turned "a 270."]
>
> **Me:** *Ooh, let's look. Put yourself right in center, and we'll do the first two steps* [of the pattern]: *step in center, step in center. And then we're going to turn to the first side* [their right] *with a jump.* [We all move together.] *And how far is that one turn?*
>
> **Kids:** *Ninety.*
>
> **Me:** *OK, it was a ninety. Who wants to tell me how they know it was a ninety-degree turn?*
>
> **Zachary:** *Because we only went to one side* [of the square].
>
> **Me:** *OK, let's do the first three beats of that pattern. Ready, go: step, step, turn side. . . . Now where are we going to end up?*
>
> **Kids:** *Back* [meaning after we do the next turn, we'll be facing the opposite side of the square, directly behind us, which is actually the left side of the square].
>
> **Me:** *Back, facing the opposite direction. Ready, go. . . . And how far did we turn on that beat?*

Video Link 2.1

In this video, a team of two boys are demonstrating their pattern A, two beats of which are 270-degree turns. I use this opportunity to reemphasize 90 degrees as the unit turn.

http://hein.pub/mathmvid2.1

Video Link 2.2

Watch two girls reason competently with turn combinations. They were really excited to show me their sequence, and with good reason. Their turn combinations were spatially complex and added a great deal to the overall choreographic effect of their final eight-beat pattern.

http://hein.pub/mathmvid2.2

Kids: *One hundred eighty.*

Me: *So why do we not call those combinations of turns 270, even though 90 and 180 do add up to 270?*

Liam: *They're two beats. You would have to do a 270 in one beat, but you did it in two beats.*

Thanks to guided conversations like these, in addition to the independent exploration children do while they create their patterns, many students become connoisseurs of rotation identification and execution. This includes being able to complete or identify a 270-degree turn or even the measurement of every rotation in a quick succession of two or three turns in the middle of an eight-beat dance pattern. Teachers have remarked that this kind of approach is also a useful way to explore cardinal directions and analog time. When rotations are used in conjunction with the moving body in math class, however, the emphasis should be firmly on the language and execution of spatial reasoning, which, as discussed earlier in the chapter, has the strongest impact on overall mathematics skills.

Part-Whole Relationships: Unitizing and Patterning

Like developing spatial and geometric reasoning, building a flexible understanding of part-whole relationships is foundational to an overall strong mathematical ability. Among other things, number sense includes understanding part-whole relationships and the myriad ways this idea presents itself, including the familiar operations of addition, subtraction, multiplication, and division as well as measurement. Sarama and Clements also include counting, comparing, unitizing, grouping, partitioning, and composing as operations (2009, 27). Many of these dynamic ideas exemplify the action side of math and are found in the realms of physical pattern creation and analysis.

Unitizing

Unitizing is the action by which the learner becomes fluent with part-whole relationships in different mathematical settings; it has parallels to learning to decode text. Learning individual letters and sounding out words eventually lead to seeing C-A-T and reading the word as a whole entity, not as its individual parts. In math, when a learner understands that smaller things can be combined to make a new, bigger thing, we call it unitizing. Like the concept of angle, the idea of unit requires multiple levels of attention from the learner. We have units of time, units of measure, and number units. How are these ideas connected? In each case there is a base unit: hours, days, inches, centimeters, and so on. In Math in Your Feet, we attend to the idea of the pattern unit: four individual actions in time that, when performed on a steady beat, can be repeated the same way each time the unit is danced. In all cases, to understand the nature of the specific unit, the learner must engage in the process of unitizing.

In his TED-Ed video "One Is One . . . or Is It?" Christopher Danielson (2012) illustrates how the idea of units and unitizing (exploring part-whole relationships) is not as straightforward as one might think. For example, *one* can mean many things, depending on the context: one bag of apples, one apple from the bag, one slice from the apple (Danielson 2012). Whether it's identifying composed units (a dozen eggs, a square made out of triangles, or 2 + 2 = 4) or partitioned units (slices of bread or division), noticing the repeated iteration of a fence post as we drive by, or executing a rhythmic pattern, we are talking about building capacity in our students to understand and usefully apply a mathematical structure that underlies all K–6 mathematics and beyond. Although we tend to think of unitizing as a process placed squarely in the domain of numbers, like many things in math, what happens in one domain shows up in other areas of math, including geometry, measurement, and patterning. Other contexts for exploring and using part-whole relationships include fractions, base ten operations, and shapes (e.g., composing a bigger triangle out of smaller triangles). In all these cases the learner needs to recognize "both the original unit and the newly composed unit simultaneously and be able to move back and forth between them seamlessly" (Danielson 2013). This is closely related to the work and thinking children do in Math in Your Feet as they create, revise, combine, and analyze four-beat foot-based pattern units. Unitizing is an important idea in a dance-making context because once you have a unit, you can take another one and put them together in interesting ways! The process of creating and performing a dance pattern unit gives children a lived, in-the-world experience with what the process of unitizing literally feels like. The process of creating a new, larger whole (in this case, combining steps into four-beat patterns and then four-beat patterns into eight-beat patterns) produces some disequilibrium in learners; it takes time and effort for them to get comfortable with the new, longer pattern, both physically and cognitively.

The Power of Patterning

Everyone benefits from learning to recognize a mathematical idea in a variety of settings. It's also clear that children benefit from having opportunities to explicitly explore the idea of mathematical patterns in multiple visual, physical, and numeric contexts. Perceptual, counting, growing, arithmetic, spatial, and geometric patterns including arrays all play a part in coming to understand the structures and processes of math as well as specific math topics. In all cases, the learner and math maker is required to "search for mathematical regularities and structures, [and] to bring order, cohesion, and predictability to seemingly unorganized situations" (Sarama and Clements 2009, 319).

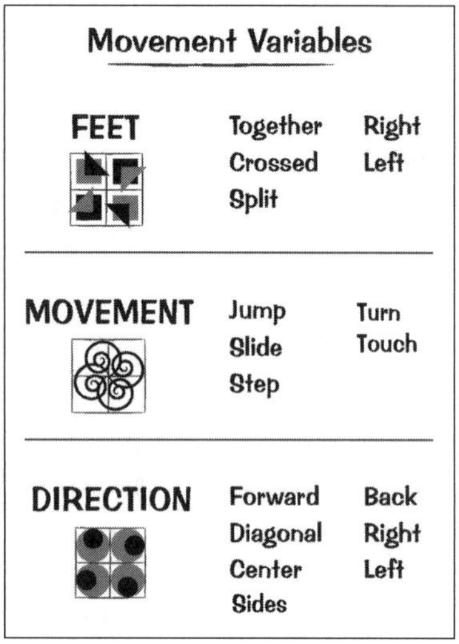

Unfortunately, when I ask fourth or fifth graders what a pattern is, I usually get an answer that hearkens back to their kindergarten experience with the idea. The fourth graders say, "Oh, you know, red, blue, red, blue," or "Circle, square, circle, square." Identifying how a pattern repeats in sequential order is fine work for kindergarten and first-grade students. However, upper-elementary students, even ones who don't seem to be "good at math," are absolutely ready to enthusiastically investigate, make, and describe patterns beyond the repetition of one attribute in a sentence-like structure.

The context for our pattern making in Math in Your Feet is an inventory of movement variables that can be combined into foot-based dance patterns: type of movement, foot position, and direction (see Figure 2.5). These three categories become the resource from which children build their choreography.

Movement Variables		
FEET	Together	Right
	Crossed	Left
	Split	
MOVEMENT	Jump	Turn
	Slide	Touch
	Step	
DIRECTION	Forward	Back
	Diagonal	Right
	Center	Left
	Sides	

▶ **Figure 2.5** Movement variables for dance patterns

Example: Unitizing, Pattern Making, and Combinations in the Primary Grades

In the following lesson a group of second graders and I took our first step down the road of understanding what it means to dance (and, eventually, make) a four-beat, foot-based dance pattern unit. I introduced two different movements—a two-footed jump (executed close to the floor) and single-footed steps (one on each foot, like marching in place), both in the center of our squares. When I saw that they were getting the gist of the patterns "jump, jump" and "step, step," I asked, "What do you think would happen if we put two jumps together and then two steps?"

Initially there was a great collective shrugging of shoulders. I asked again: "What do you think would happen?" A boy in the back ventured an answer:

Boy: *Um, it will be four?*

Me: [Thinking about units] *It will be four what?*

Boy: *It will be four . . . movements.*

Me: *Ah, four movements! What else could it be four of? Is there any other way to describe the four?*

Girl in back: *It could be a rhythm.*

Me: *It could be a four . . . what do we call what makes the rhythm?*

Girl: *Beats?*

Me: *Yeah, a four-beat rhythm. Let's try it together.* [Burst of inspiration] *Actually, do you guys just want to see what two jumps and two steps look like and feel like? I'll walk around and watch what you're doing.*

After giving the class a couple of minutes to work with the task, I paused the dancing and asked, "Who wants to show me 'jump, jump, step, step'?" I had *assumed* that because I had asked what would happen if they put two jumps and two steps together, I would get a single answer, with the movements in the order in which I had mentioned them in the question. Silly me.

Student: *Can we do any pattern?*

Me: Any *pattern? Did you come up with something else?*

Student: *Yeah: "jump, step, jump, step."*

I walked over to our little whiteboard (as pictured in Figure 2.6) and said, "Wow. You know what? It's not up here on this board. These patterns are from the first graders [earlier in the day], and look! Now I have a fourth pattern to put on here. You guys dance it, and we'll say it and dance it with our hands while we're sitting." Everyone chanted with me, "Jump, step, jump, step," while at the same time rehearsing the steps with their hands. Still on my agenda of getting the answer I was looking for, I asked: "Who else wants to show what they've done? Who has JJSS?" After a team of two boys showed us this combination, I asked, "Who would like to play around with some ideas about different ways to combine jumps and steps?" All hands went up, the kids jumped up, and the whole class started working in their teams of two.

The class continued to experiment with different combinations of jumps and steps and had, in just thirty minutes, become familiar with a new kind of pattern unit, one built with the elements of time, space, and body. They had experienced how steps and jumps could be sequenced and resequenced to create a variety of new dance patterns and had experienced the idea of pattern unit as a dynamic object, open to manipulation, experimentation, and investigation. A playful, creative experience with a personally relevant mathematical object like a dance pattern unit supports the development of flexible mathematical thinking and problem solving. Also see Figure 2.7.

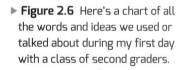

Malke
tap dancing   middle
clogging   center
. rhythm   jump
  Pattern   step
  ⓠ JJSS   touch
  ② JSSJ ③ JJTT
  ②₁₀₀ SSSS ④ JSJS

▶ **Figure 2.6** Here's a chart of all the words and ideas we used or talked about during my first day with a class of second graders.

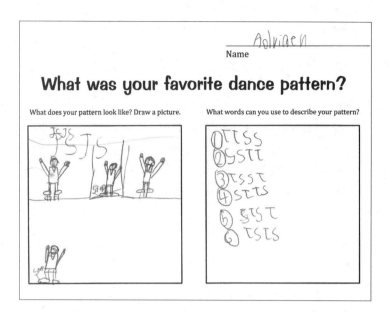

▶ **Figure 2.7** This second grader recorded her favorite dance pattern for the day in pictorial form and, on the right, recorded all the different combinations of jumps and steps the class danced that day.

Equivalence Relations and Comparisons: Thinking About Sameness, Similarity, Difference, and Change

After a few years of work developing Math in Your Feet, I began to wonder: *What other kinds of math are the children making and using beyond patterns and specific geometry concepts?* I found my answer one day when I was playing with tangram shapes alongside my then six-year-old daughter. In our case we had mixed a bunch of sets together so we had many different colors to work with while we created a collaborative design. I was trying to talk about what we were doing as we played and suddenly it hit me—we were discussing the attributes of the different pieces, comparing the size, shape, and color of one piece with others within the design. This kind of activity and discussion is a core math skill, essentially the ability to discern similarities, differences, and sameness, also known as equivalence relations. In this case we were not just evaluating congruence (a geometry concept that is present when the properties of geometric objects are exactly the same when compared with each other) but also engaging in a dynamic mathematical activity of sorting and comparing the shapes to find similarities and differences.

Equivalence is a tool for assessing mathematical relationships and an overarching idea that includes equality (numerical sameness), similarity, and congruence (geometric sameness). In all three of these situations the goal is to decide which properties to focus on and then evaluate those aspects of things or ideas to determine whether they fit our definition of equivalent. In our case, the triangle-shaped puzzle pieces were three different sizes and three different colors. Which one of those properties (also known as attributes) should we use when comparing them—size or color? A small yellow triangle and a larger yellow triangle could be similar if we focused on the shared attribute yellow. Whatever rule we made, something mathematicians do all the time, would be our definition of equivalence. This kind of building and comparing is at the heart of the mathematical activity in our math-and-dance making.

Using Variables and Attributes in a Making Context

The movement variables I mentioned earlier are not variables in the algebraic sense, although they will be things that vary. They are actually *categorical variables*, which help us describe, sort, and analyze data that are not necessarily ordered. For example, when comparing colors, which comes first—brown or red? Does curly hair come before straight? Categories like hair color or type of pet cannot be put in any particular order. Categorical variables also lend themselves very well to a making process, providing a structure for flexible choice making and experimentation in the process of creating something new, like a dance pattern! Our dance patterns have the categorical variables of foot position, movement, and direction. Within each of those three categories lies an inventory of choices for the math-and-dance maker. Whether we're in the process of creating or analyzing our own or others' dance patterns, we use these categories to help us focus our attention on particular properties of the dance pattern under analysis. For example, you can describe or evaluate a dance pattern using only *movement words*:

jump, jump, jump, slide

Alternately, focusing on *foot position*, this pattern could be described like this:

split, cross, split, together

Finally, you could name the *directions* in which the team moves on each beat:

sides, center, sides, center

Video Link 2.3

For this demonstration, I asked whether this team's eight-beat pattern was composed of "two different (four-beat) patterns or two of the same." See what you think, and then listen to two boys as they provide reasons for their answers.

http://hein.pub/mathmvid2.3

Video Link 2.4

In this video, the class had been working on creating their pattern A, and the demonstration team provided us with some useful fodder for discussing sameness between teammates.

http://hein.pub/mathmvid2.4

Equivalence: Examining Sameness

Initially, my reasons for focusing children's attention on these individual categories was to help them become more aware of what they were doing and the decisions they were making while they choreographed their steps. It worked! They danced so much more clearly and precisely once the language was made explicit. But there was also an amazing mathematical consequence as well. When the categories became more explicit for my students, they were better able to reason about sameness as they compared one dance pattern with another.

When we explore sameness in the dance work, we focus on the question *How are these two patterns the same?* This is a great question especially if the two patterns look radically different from each other. Two patterns may use the same movements but be different in every other way. In the end, clarifying the different categories provides a framework for both an artistic analysis of the work and a mathematical analysis of the patterns themselves.

Another question around sameness in the dance is this: *What does it mean to dance the same as your partner?* To answer this question, students need to compare two objects, in this case the patterns created by two moving dancers. When asked how they knew they were dancing the same as their partner, students most often mentioned watching each other to see if their feet were in the same places in the square. This is a great start, but they also need to focus their attention on the ideas of direction and the type of movement they are using. The conversations between partners around the adjustments that need to happen to make sure they are dancing the same pattern the same way require the team to execute the dance moves precisely to show their understanding. This, in turn, brings them much closer to understanding what sameness and congruence mean in relation to another person's dancing.

Example: Making and Comparing Difference

The flip side of sameness is difference. The process of creating a second four-beat pattern completely different from the first is not as easy as it might seem. To *make difference*, students need to compare their first pattern with their plan for their second pattern. For example, kids often start their choreography with a pattern full of jumps. To create difference, and indeed choreographic variety and contrast, they can look at their other movement choices to find other options for moving around the square (step, slide, touch). Or, if they have a bunch of turns in the first pattern, the second should have none. Other children take the challenge by the horns and start their second pattern somewhere other than center—facing the diagonal, perhaps, or standing at the back of their square. Sometimes kids will switch boxes with their partner mid-dance. Ultimately, making *difference* the challenge for the second pattern gives students a chance to try out new movements, directions, and foot positions they might not have explored otherwise. It also forces them (in a good way!) to compare their two patterns. *Are they different enough from each other? How do you know? What is different between A and B? What things are similar or exactly the same?*

In a conversation about mathematical sameness with my colleague Christopher Danielson, he said, "A fundamental characteristic of mathematical activity is when you say *exactly* what it is you want to pay attention to and focus only on that attribute and ignore everything else." In Math in Your Feet students do exactly this in an incredibly fluid way through conversation with their partners and physical problem solving. Within just a five- or ten-minute period, they often flexibly and enthusiastically evaluate the attributes of their first pattern, choose and experiment with new attributes, and decide when they've made pattern B different enough to meet the criteria I've provided. And they do it all while analyzing and executing moving patterns in real time. Every single aspect of this process is mathematical and encourages the development of the kinds of fluid and competent reasoning we want from our students in any math learning context.

Video Link 2.5

This video allows us to listen in as two girls puzzle out what it might mean to make their pattern B different from their pattern A.

http://hein.pub/mathmvid2.5

Example: Exploring Similarity and Change with Transformations

Once we've established the understanding of sameness in the dancing, we move on to transformation, which requires further comparison between the patterns danced by a team of two students and creates a dynamic setting for exploring reflection symmetry. Students often encounter reflection symmetry in a static, visual form, generally by drawing a line of symmetry through the middle of an object or between two objects. If the object is the same on both sides of that line, it is said to be reflected or have reflection symmetry. However, this will not get you all the way to understanding the concept. Anna Sfard wrote, "Symmetry can be conceived as a static property of geometric form but also as a kind of transformation" (1991, 15). This idea is very similar to our discussion of the concept of angle earlier in this chapter. Symmetry can be conceived *either* as an object *or* an action that produces the symmetry: to understand what a reflection is, we need to experience it in both its static form and as the dynamic process that creates that image. "For all the attention and respect given to the [static] approach," Sfard writes, "the [action] mode of thinking will also get its due share . . . a profound insight into the processes underlying mathematical concepts, maybe even a certain degree of mastery in performing these processes, *should sometimes be viewed as a basis for understanding such concepts rather than as its outcome*" (1991, 15; emphasis mine).

Dancing a transformation requires the learner to think closely about what she needs to do (or not do) to create a dance pattern that includes both dancers and exhibits the reflection symmetry. We naturally focus as much on the process of transformation, the action that *produces* the resulting symmetry, as on the result. The two dancers have to think of themselves in one of two roles: either the original or the reflection. The reflection has the challenge of physically enacting changes to the dancing; specifically, this means doing the opposite rights and lefts of the original, in both footwork and directions. For the audience, this provides rich opportunities to analyze whether the dance team really did perform their pattern with reflection or not, and why. These are some of our favorite moments in Math in Your Feet and also moments that are ripe with opportunity to notice and assess what your students understand about transformations and symmetries simply by observing their dancing and listening to their responses.

I often ask individual teams or the class as a whole, *How do you know that that pattern was reflected?* To answer this question, students must assess the similarity in the pattern as danced by both dancers. This requires the development of some cognitive flexibility when determining sameness. Both partners' feet may be near the line of reflection (one interpretation of sameness), but they are also in opposite positions in relation to each other (a dancer's *right* foot is toward the line and her partner's *left* foot is toward that line). Evaluating the similarity between two patterns requires students to use precise language that then helps them clarify the footwork of others as well as their own.

Mathematical Thinking and Sense Making

At its core, mathematical thinking is the ultimate mathematical verb, with the potential to engage students in personally relevant sense making. Sense making includes, but is not limited to, engaging in conversations, experimenting, puzzling out, thinking beyond the algorithm, making connections, using mathematical language in context, considering others' strategies, and developing new strategies. The dynamic math topics and concepts depicted in this chapter have shown the rich, vibrant thinking and reasoning needed to learn, understand, and enjoy mathematics. Exploring math with the moving body provides children with the opportunity to get a feel for, and a memorable experience with, the structures, relationships, and processes that they also need when they encounter math in other settings. This happens because the physical challenges themselves create a potent environment for engaging in mathematical sense making, thinking, and problem solving, and they make visible that there are certain attitudes, dispositions, and ways of thinking that, when applied and developed over time, can help students become competent problem solvers. In turn, these dispositions can help students develop a better understanding of the concepts and reasoning behind the content and apply that understanding in new and novel situations.

The Standards for Mathematical Practice from the Common Core State Standards summarize some of these key dispositions and processes. Four of those practices are especially relevant to the kind of math-and-dance learning I discuss in this book: practice 1, "Make sense of problems and persevere in solving them"; practice 5, "Use appropriate tools strategically"; practice 6, "Attend to precision"; and practice 7, "Look for and make use of structure" (NGA Center for Best Practices and CCSSO 2010, 6–8).

Make Sense of Problems and Persevere in Solving Them

Perseverance in the face of the unknown can be a big hill to climb in mathematical problem solving. It means being okay with ambiguity while you work to make sense of the mathematical challenge in front of you, at least for a little while. This perseverance is also a necessary mind-set for finding answers to questions for which you do not yet know how to find an answer. Having observed literally thousands of elementary kids working their way through a math-and-dance challenge to create something brand-new, I know there are definitely moments where the process "stalls" and children are not really sure which way to turn, both literally and figuratively. What makes the biggest difference in moving past moments of "stuckness" is the fact that the math-and-dance making is by nature a highly personal activity. The process is personal because students are given agency over their decisions and behavior; they have control over everything except the constraint of having a final eight-beat pattern danced in a two-by-two-foot square. They possess this agency from the beginning, when the teacher introduces them to a tool kit of resources from which to choose and a partner on whom to rely. The teacher then supports them in their efforts by offering a series of small, open-ended tasks. It's the synergy between all of these elements that activates their personal investment in the process to power them through when things get tough or confusing.

Use Appropriate Tools Strategically

Along with the movement variables, students' tools and resources in this work include their partners, the square dance spaces themselves, and their observations of others' work (which can both help put their own work into perspective and serve as creative inspiration). By having agency over their tool choice and their decision-making process (including judgements about when they think their pattern is done), they are getting a feel for what it means to evaluate a variety of strategies (a wonderful meta-tool) and apply them in ways that influence their final product in beneficial ways. This often occurs in multiple iterations of trial and error. I usually notice big gains in effective tool use when kids make their second four-beat pattern, which indicates that they have developed a good feel for and understanding of when and how to use all the tools, explicit and implicit, at their disposal.

Attend to Precision

Thinking mathematically means, in part, thinking about and expressing a mathematical idea concisely in both words and symbols. "Attending to precision" means focusing on the appropriate details in a task in order to make progress in finding a solution. It also means communicating your mathematical ideas precisely. Developmentally, elementary students are still traveling toward precision in thought, language, and deed. In both moving-scale and math-and-dance settings, this process is supported and improved through the use of precise language in partnership with a specific body task.

The precise expression of a precise dance form in multiple expressive modes (physical, verbal, and visual) is a visceral benchmark of what it means to think and articulate oneself precisely in a mathematical context. Precision in thought, word, and deed is also required in nondance moving-scale challenges. In Chapter 3 I share the story of fourth graders who felt quite strongly that, because of an in-depth inquiry into the topic the previous year, they knew pretty much everything about polygons. However, when presented with the unusual context of a twelve-foot rope divided into one-foot intervals and the task of working in small groups to create as many different regular polygons as they could, they were well challenged by the change of scale and mode. The collaborative moving-scale construction itself necessitated precise thinking and communication to others in their group as they negotiated different conceptions of how to create "equal sides." This task required clear communication between groupmates to negotiate multiple interpretations of the challenge in question and to determine how to use the rope most accurately in solving the challenge.

Look for and Make Use of Structure

As discussed earlier in this chapter, part-whole relationships make up the structure around which much of elementary math learning is based. The experience of creating seemingly simple dance pattern units, especially in the primary grades, creates a potent opportunity for exploring and deepening understanding of this concept alongside the many other ways we harness the relationship between parts and wholes while learning math. Exploring part-whole relationships with the whole body has the potential to help students strengthen and deepen their understanding of the concept.

In this chapter I have zoomed in closely on the kinds of math learned when the whole, moving body is harnessed as an object to think with in a mathematical context. Don't forget, though, that this kind of approach is not just about the math; it's the *partnership between* the math and the whole, moving body that creates opportunities for potent mathematical sense making. In the rest of this book I detail specific activities, starting in the next chapter with low-stakes, nondance activities as well as some more formally facilitated lessons, all of which can give you a sense of what it feels, looks, and sounds like to engage your students in mathematical sense making by engaging their whole, moving bodies.

Chapter Three

Beyond Mnemonics
Getting Started with Moving-Scale Math

If the whole, moving body in math learning is best conceived as a thinking tool as opposed to a mnemonic device, what are the alternatives to making up routines to memorize your times tables or the area of a circle? And what's the best way for a teacher to get started? The lessons and activities in this chapter were designed to provide answers to both questions. I've structured this chapter sort of like a zero-entry swimming pool. You can start at the shallow end and get your feet wet by incorporating students' whole bodies into familiar math activities you might already be doing at hand or desk scale. Or, if you feel ready, you can jump into the deep end and facilitate a more organized activity. This is not about replacing an entire math unit with moving-scale, body-based learning or changing your teaching approach overnight. Instead, this is a chance to get a sense of what it feels, looks, and sounds like to engage your students in mathematical sense making by engaging their whole, moving bodies in collaboration with other learners.

The activities in this chapter are labeled with suggested grade levels but are appropriate for a grade or two above or below the identified grade band. You know your students, their struggles, and their strengths. If neither you nor your students have tried anything like this before, my advice is to embrace the newness as a class community. Enlist your students as coinvestigators as you embark on a grand experiment. Model a can-do-even-though-it's-new attitude and ask them to join you in the adventure. Afterward, ask them how things went and what might make the lesson easier to understand the next time you do it with a group of students.

Moving Off the Page: Changing the Scale of the Math You're Already Doing

September 2014 found Jenn Kranenburg, a relatively new elementary teacher in Ontario, Canada, at a new school teaching a class of grades 2 and 3 students and spending a great deal of time addressing undesirable student behaviors. She quickly realized this was because she was asking students to do something that many were not capable of: sit still and quietly for extended periods of time. She decided to integrate more opportunities for movement during the school day and hoped that this change would redirect both her and her students' energy away from managing behaviors and toward increased participation in learning.

Jenn noticed immediate gains when she replaced a round table and chairs with two standing tables and turned a wall of high shelves into standing work space. Not only did all students give greater attention to tasks, but she also spent less time redirecting students, and the community as a whole experienced fewer disruptions. Seeing such positive results from a small change motivated her to continue to explore how she could provide more opportunities for whole-body engagement during the school day.

Math was one of the areas she focused on during this transition. "I understand from my own schooling what it is like to have anxiety around math and to struggle with concepts and vocabulary. So, I decided to approach my teaching in a way that would have made sense to me when I was in elementary school," Jenn said. She began moving math off the page with her measurement strand. She started an indoor garden, and children tracked and compared the growth of plants. She also incorporated cooking into math time and set up a precipitation gauge in front of the school as a registered weather station, all of which provided students with the opportunity to get up and move around while supporting the development of their mathematical sense making. Because students were responding favorably to these changes, Jenn was inspired to look for other ways (detailed in this section) to include her students' whole bodies in their math learning. They are all wonderful, useful, and low-stress possible first steps in bringing moving-scale math learning into your classroom. Jenn told me, "I know teachers might have anxiety about an approach like mine. There seems to be a misconception that learning requires a silent classroom with students filling in worksheets. Instead, I focus on the on the verbs in the curriculum: *explore, create, construct, compare, measure, solve*—all things we can do out of our seats." As described in Chapter 2, the verbs of math are exactly what we need to focus on when we partner a moving body with a math investigation.

Incorporating the Whole, Moving Body in Daily Math Lessons

After some opening warm-up routines, Jenn poses a problem, the class as a whole brainstorms possible ways to solve the problem, and then everyone goes off to work on it in small groups or individually. The children choose strategies that make the most sense to them, and over time, they have come to understand that using their bodies is a viable and sometimes highly effective option.

For example, consider this problem:

> Sam wants to find friends to play a game. His friends live on his side of the street. First he goes down the hill four houses to get Tara, who lives in the first house on the block. Then he goes up the hill six houses to get Frank. From there he goes down the hill three houses to find Karly. Next he goes up the hill thirteen houses to find Laura. Laura lives in the last house on the street. How many houses are on the street in total?

As the students discussed possible strategies for solving the problem, some decided to draw a diagram to help them work out an answer but quickly got confused with where they left off and the direction in which they were headed. One group decided to use their bodies to represent the students in the story. They agreed on where the bottom of the hill would be and used chairs to represent the houses. Students then took the roles of the people in the problem and enacted it, moving themselves and the chairs as needed. It was much easier for them to complete the activity accurately, as opposed to the other students, who struggled to complete the task in twenty minutes. Some students who had opted to use pencil and paper realized the success of the moving-scale strategy and decided to get up and act out the problem as well.

Measurement: Using Bodies to Measure, Compare, and Estimate Length and Weight

Measurement is more than the act of measuring. It's about comparing, estimating, and interpreting data to make sense of a particular situation. "We have a scale in our room and use our bodies to measure, compare, and estimate length and weight," Jenn said. "We also use our bodies as benchmarks for measuring other items." During an investigation about a pumpkin's weight, for example, Jenn's students wondered how much it weighed.

Almost immediately, Jenn said, "Little Jayden was thrown into the equation [what a great sport she is!], and she was lifted and compared with the weight of the pumpkin." Jayden's classmates asked her to step on the classroom scale, and then they used her known weight to make reasonable estimations about the weight of the pumpkin. Quickly, they all wanted to know their own weights, so they all stood on the scale and then decided to stand in line from lightest to heaviest, which led to their realization that height is not always an indicator of weight. (Johnny was taller than Mariah but also lighter.) "My experience with primary students," Jenn said, "is that they are highly egocentric, so making math about them makes it so much more engaging; engaging their whole body in the process is one way to do this."

Jenn again harnessed her students' bodies as tools for making sense of the massive amount of snow that had accumulated during a giant storm. Students measured out the total height of the snowfall with a piece of tape and then taped it to their bodies to see how deep the snow was compared with their own height. Would it go up to their knees? To their waists? To their chests?

The Many Uses of a Body-Scale Hundred Chart

When thinking about helping her students develop number sense with their whole bodies, Jenn decided to create an enlarged, body-scale version of a hundred chart that was large enough for everyone to sit around and have a good view of during instruction and activities. To create the hundred chart on her floor, Jenn used the floor tiles as a guide. Each square was five by five inches, resulting in a grid that measured a little over four by four feet. (Painters tape works better for marking out such a grid than duct tape, which is very hard to remove.) The hundred chart was located on the classroom floor, in an area that did not have heavy traffic. While it could be covered by a table and chairs if needed, students preferred to have it accessible at all times, so that they could use it during their free time. That year Jenn devoted a good amount of time to developing a sense of what she calls "howmuchness" in number, with some children moving on the body-scale hundred grid while the rest used whiteboard versions to follow along with the action. Here are some examples of how she and her students explored number concepts and relationships and symmetry, all on the same body-scale hundred grid.

Finding Number Patterns and Relationships (grades K–4)

Before Jenn created the body-scale hundred chart, she had been exploring number concepts using ten-by-ten-inch whiteboard charts. She had the students place a token on the chart and then move the token ten spaces.

"My hope was that the students would recognize that simply moving down one space, to the next row, would result in adding ten to a number; however, only two students recognized this," she said. Jenn decided to move the task to the hundred chart on the floor to see if it might help student understanding. She began with the same number as before, asking Johnny to stand on the three and Alexis to move ten spaces from Johnny. She moved forward seven spaces to get to the ten and then went to the beginning of the next row and moved forward another three spaces to end at the thirteen. Jenn told me that Alexis immediately looked at Johnny and said, "Hey, we're standing next to each other!" They repeated the activity with different numbers, and students began to realize that "all [they] really needed to do, to add ten to a number on a hundred chart, [was] move down one row," and that all that was changing was that they "were adding one on the tens column." "When children were moving the tokens on the hundred chart," Jenn said, "some struggled with carrying over the tokens from the end of the first row to the beginning of the tens column, resulting in an incorrect ending space. Others just didn't seem to recognize the pattern. When their whole bodies were engaged, however, they appeared to take more care in the accuracy of their movements. Students exhibited more control over ensuring that their bodies remained in the proper space, whereas they seemed to not recognize inaccuracies in a smaller space."

Exploring Symmetry with the Body and with Shapes on the Hundred Chart (grades 2–5)

Jenn also used the hundred chart to help her students explore symmetry concepts. "We started by using our bodies," Jenn said. "We marked a line of symmetry on the hundred chart. Students were asked to lie down so that their body was on the line of symmetry correctly. Some students initially placed their body so the line was dividing them at their waist. They quickly realized that this didn't make sense and would move their body so the line was travelling down the center of their body. They then moved on to reflections, translations, and rotations and would 'slide' from one segment of the grid to another and turn so their feet remained in the same spot, but the rest of their body was facing in a new direction. Rileigh was the first student to participate in this activity and she had a hard time differentiating between a translation and rotation. I asked her to lie on the grid and then had her slide her entire body the same distance. Next I asked her to keep her feet positioned in the same spot, but to turn the rest of her body, so she was facing in a different position, to show a rotation of her body. Going through this process with her whole body was exactly what Rileigh needed to come to terms with what the math terminology was describing." The students took turns using their bodies to show each of the movements and challenged their classmates to identify a given movement as a translation, reflection, or rotation. "When we went to the tables to explore these transformations with pattern blocks, all students had a firm understanding of how to slide, flip, or turn a block," Jenn said. One of the reasons this kind of activity worked so well for Jenn's students is that the chart on the floor created a frame in which to orient the activity. In Chapter 2, I focused on the need for being able to track the starting location of a rotation all the way through to the ending position. The hundred chart provided a similar context for transformations.

Jenn's class also completed and described images that had vertical, horizontal, or diagonal lines of symmetry. Students used painters tape to make lines of symmetry and then used shapes made out of tagboard, which replicated the pattern blocks they used at hand scale, to fill in one half of the grid with a design and then have their peers complete the other half. The children loved this activity so much that it became a favorite rainy-day recess activity in their room.

Jenn's approach to incorporating her students' whole bodies in their math investigations models all of the criteria for moving-scale math learning as outlined at the beginning of Chapter 1. "This approach has helped my students not only to develop a deeper understanding of mathematical concepts," Jenn told me, "but also to change their mind-set toward math. The learning that occurs through rich tasks that allow for movement, math talk, exploration, risk taking, and opportunities for multiple strategies have resulted in the development of a community of learners who are excited to tackle every challenge presented to them. The greatest reward for me is that this gives all students, regardless of their ability level, the opportunity to learn, be successful, and *enjoy* math class."

Providing New Perspectives on Number and Geometry

When we move in and through space, we are thinking and reasoning both spatially and geometrically. The shortcut through an empty lot is often a beaten-down path on the diagonal, the shortest distance across. Playground swings give us a visceral sense of curved space as they arc us from high point to high point. Street intersections are places of directional decision making: Which way should we go? What is the quickest route? So it makes sense that we will naturally arrive at geometry as a useful and meaningful pairing between the whole, moving body and mathematics. What we want to avoid, however, is a literal reenactment of how we already know and understand geometric ideas on the page. No one representation gives the full picture, and we need to remain curious about what new perspectives the body and a change of scale can bring to the investigation. This section describes and illustrates how humble and inexpensive materials like painters tape and clothesline, in partnership with students' bodies and an explicit mathematical challenge, can expand students' perspectives in ways that bring the numeric and geometric together, engage them in potent problem solving, and expand and deepen their understanding of seemingly familiar mathematics. See this in action in Figures 3.1–3.3.

SCALING UP: BIGGER THAN A PIECE OF PAPER

(30–40 minutes; grades K–2)

▶ **Figure 3.1**

This activity changes the scale of a familiar investigation of polygons and allows young children the opportunity to create geometric objects at body scale. Using blue painters tape encourages the enlargement of line and intersection. The collaborative nature of "drawing" shapes with tape requires students to negotiate a shared vision of form and size with their partners. Jointly constructing a shape one piece of tape at a time slows down the thinking process and creates opportunities for conversations between partners about both their mathematical and creative intentions. Finally, we should not underestimate the learning opportunities generated by an active making process for evaluating strategy and outcomes, as well as using and modeling mathematical and spatial terminology in context.

Math: Scale; compare and contrast; model shapes in the world by drawing shapes and building them from components and with defining attributes; use relational language; compose two-dimensional shapes; create composite shapes

Materials: Low-tack painters tape, children's safety scissors

Space: Enough open space so every group of two can make a shape bigger than a sheet of paper

Lesson Progression

1. Open the lesson by asking the students about what kinds of shapes they can think of or what shapes they can see around them in the classroom.

▶ Figure 3.2

▶ Figure 3.3

2. Give the class the challenge to "make a shape bigger than a piece of paper" with tape on the floor, and provide some guidance about the materials (blue painters tape and a pair of scissors). Also, give clear expectations for and ideas about how to work peacefully with a partner on this project.

3. Have teams of two (or three, maximum) pick an area of floor space and work together to create a shape on the floor with the tape. As they work, observe and monitor the activity, and talk with individual groups about their efforts.

4. Pause the action when each group has created at least one taped shape, and facilitate conversations about the children's making process. Listen to the language students are using and model mathematical and spatial language in the context of the conversation and activity.

5. Send students back to work with a challenge based on this conversation that encourages them to fully embrace and explore the possibilities of creating shapes that are bigger than a sheet of paper.

Extending the Learning

For further geometric explorations, children can play freely with pattern blocks or go on a "shape walk" to look for shapes inside and out and then make a record of their discoveries. In a more guided exploration, children can connect the geometry to numbers by composing individual shapes using straight objects, such as pencils or sticks. What do they notice about the different shapes? Which aspects are the same? Which aspects are different? What parts of a shape are countable? Making a graph or table of this information with your students will help students make comparisons between the shapes. You can also play "Which One Doesn't Belong?" ("WODB?"), an open-ended activity that promotes comparisons and conversations around sameness and difference. More information about "WODB?" can be found in Chapter 8.

Opening and Tracking the Lesson

The premise for this lesson is straightforward: "When we draw shapes, often they can get only as big as a piece of paper. Today we're going to make shapes that are *bigger* than a piece of paper, and not only that, they'll be made out of tape. You and your partner will get a roll of tape and a pair of scissors. You're going to decide with your partner about what shape you want to make and how much bigger than a piece of paper you want to make it."

Of course kids will start thinking and talking immediately about what they want to make, which can lead to some interesting conversations. Notice how the following conversation (with a group of K–1 students) naturally shifted to the ubiquitous nature of shapes. We want to encourage this kind of thinking and observation because the more we are able to recognize math ideas in a variety of settings and contexts, the more easily we can build and maintain a positive relationship to mathematics as a useful and relevant subject.

Clara: *I'm going to make a skinny rectangle!*

Me: *Yeah! So you can start thinking about what kind of shape you might want to make.*

Isabel: *And shapes have sides.*

Me: *Can you tell me more about that?*

Isabel: *Yeah. Like squares and rectangles have four sides. And also triangles have three sides because it has a point right here* [pointing to an imaginary vertex in the vicinity of her face].

Lydia: *This is a comment. If we decide to make a circle or something, I prefer not to do that.*

Me: *OK. So you've already made some decisions about how you'd like you and your partner to work?*

Lydia: *Yes.*

Eli: *Pretty much everything is a shape.*

Me: *Can you say more about that?*

Eli: *Like, this room, I'm pretty sure is a* [looking around the room] . . .

[Maria traces the floor to the wall to the ceiling to the wall, in the air.]

Kids interrupt: *It's full of shapes. It's square.*

Eli: [Continuing] *. . . probably all rectangles. And, like, that bookshelf—it's a rectangle. And the other bookshelf—it's also rectangle.*

Isabel: *Circles have no sides.*

Me: *Why do you say that?*

Isabel: *Because they're round.*

Leah: *And that tape is round. And doughnuts are circles with a hole in the middle that's also a circle.*

Students got started and worked diligently for about ten minutes. Once I saw that a majority of teams were getting close to being finished, I let the whole class know that we would be pausing the action in a minute to look at what others had made.

One aspect of learning math at moving scale is that orientation is relative to the viewer. For example, in elementary contexts we often see equilateral triangles with one edge parallel to the bottom edge of a piece of paper. When you are used to seeing triangles in this way, a similar triangle in a different context or orientation might seem unfamiliar. This conundrum was illustrated during our gallery walk (as we walked around the room to view the teams' shapes):

Sophia: *I noticed that it has three sides.*

Audrey: *I noticed that it has a pointed top and it has a bottom like a triangle.*

Zachary: *I noticed that it's like, pointed on, like, the bottom, like that way.*

Me: [To Zachary] *Oh, interesting! Audrey noticed that the "top" was there* [the vertex in a standard orientation of a triangle]. *And you noticed that the top was there. . . . And, look, you're standing in different places.*

Sophia: *I think this is the top.*

Audrey: *No,* this *is the top.*

Me: *And look where you're standing; you're each seeing different things. Interesting!*

Presenting a Challenge

The results of the gallery walk with the kindergarten and first-grade group revealed that they, on the whole, had created shapes out of tape that were approximately the size of a sheet of paper. I reiterated the goal for creating shapes that were "*bigger* than a sheet of paper" and let them get back to work. It soon became evident that most teams were focusing on finding ways to enlarge their original shape. The test of "bigger" turned out to be whether or not one or both partners could fit inside the taped shape. Most groups approached this goal by taping down longer segments of tape, like Group 1 did (as illustrated in Figures 3.4, 3.5, and 3.6). You can see in the figures how the boys in Group 1 compared the sizes of their own bodies with the shapes they constructed and added a semi-narrative context (calling his tape triangles "teeth") to the activity, as primary students are wont to do.

Me: [To Ryder] *What's your idea here?*

Ryder: *Well, I have an idea for teeth.* (See Figure 3.4.)

Asher (Ryder's teammate): *I wanted to make a big rectangle.* (See Figure 3.5)

Classroom teacher: *It's big enough you can be inside it!*

Asher: *A lot of people could be inside of it!* (See Figure 3.6.)

▶ **Figure 3.4**

▶ **Figure 3.5**

▶ **Figure 3.6**

Group 2, on the other hand, started by creating a triangle much smaller than a piece of paper. Instead of expanding the shape by making it bigger, they added more small triangles and some squares, and also created a larger rectangle around the triangles, leaving evidence of their thinking about how smaller shapes can be combined to make larger shapes. You can see what they did in Figures 3.7, 3.8, and 3.9.

> **Aiden (pointing):** *This was our first triangle.*
>
> **Me:** *OK, and then what did you do?*
>
> **Evan:** *Then we did this big rectangle and then we put two triangles and then we did this* [made individual "squares"].
>
> **Aiden:** *And now we're going to put one on this side.* (See Figure 3.8.)
>
> **Me:** *And what would you call this shape?*
>
> **Evan:** *A square with no end . . .*
>
> **Me:** *Could this become its end* [pointing to the side of the large rectangle]?
>
> **Evan:** *Yeah, this could be part of the square and the rectangle.*
>
> **Me:** *Yeah, you could have a shared side.*

Group 3 started with a square. Then they added onto it to create a large rectangle. (See Figures 3.10 and 3.11.)

> **Me:** *Can I ask you what your plan was here? What did you want to make?*
>
> **Partners:** *Something really big!*
>
> **Me:** *OK. See if you can fill your shape with your whole body! See if both partners can fill your shape. Can you get inside your shape?*

▶ **Figure 3.7** Evan making his "square with no end."

▶ **Figure 3.8** Adding more squares to the outside of the rectangle

▶ **Figure 3.9** The boys started by taping a small triangle. Here they are trying to figure out if they've made it big enough for both of them to get inside it.

Exploring the construction of shapes by changing the scale and drawing medium is a potent starting point both for assessing current student conceptions around geometric forms and for providing a visceral experience with scale. When students interact with polygons in a way that requires them to be the makers of salient attributes such as edges, corners (vertices), and angles, they begin to explore and experience aspects of the shapes in ways they hadn't when simply identifying shapes on the page in visual form. Not only is fitting yourself *inside* a shape a new and utterly novel experience, but the relationship of those two corners of the square is now viscerally represented by your body (see Figure 3.12).

In this activity, the initial in-the-moment conversations should be focused on what the children did to make their shapes. Leave the second round of more mathematical conversations for a later time (though if mathematical thoughts arise, it's OK to go with the flow!). To do this, take photos of all the shapes made with tape. When you are ready to revisit the activity, project the photos for the whole class to see and spend some time noticing and wondering (see Chapter 4 of Ray 2013) about what the class made. You might begin to see shared attributes between seemingly diverse constructions, which might prompt an interesting conversation focused on making comparisons and conjectures about the nature of polygons.

▶ **Figure 3.10** Group 3's initial shape.

▶ **Figure 3.12** Group 4 proving that their bodies can fill their shape. Notice the boy stretching his feet toward the bottom two corners of their "house."

▶ **Figure 3.11** Group 3's expanded shape.

PROVING CENTER

(30–45 minutes; grades K–2)

In this activity, children work collaboratively in teams of three to five to determine the "center" of a taped, ladderlike structure on the floor. Although teams may solve the initial challenge rather quickly, the core mathematical experience is in having each group prove that it has found the right location. The mathematical ideas of center, middle, and half are related in ways that create a powerful overlap between the numeric and geometric aspects of math, creating potential for further rich explorations of these ideas both on and off the page.

▶ **Figure 3.13**

Math: Developing multiple conceptions of *half*; exploring symmetry; distinguishing between even and odd numbers; considering sameness and equality; employing one-to-one correspondence in a new context; expressing the length of an object as a whole number of length units; partitioning a rectangle into rows and columns of same-size squares and counting to find the total number of them; attending to precision; looking for and making use of structure; reasoning quantitatively; constructing viable arguments.

Materials and dimensions: The ladders are twenty-five feet long and eleven inches wide (see Figure 3.13). You'll need blue, low-tack painters tape to make one structure for each group of four or five, leaving some space around each. I constructed mine using the cracks in a gym floor to help keep the outside lines of tape straight, and then used a piece of 8½-by-11-inch paper to measure out twenty-five cells. I positioned two ladders opposite each other so that their cells matched up with each other, though this orientation is not crucial to the activity. The only specific requirement is that a single child could stand inside an individual cell; do what you need to do to make it work in your space!

Space: Enough space for all the ladders with room in between. An LGI (large-group instruction) room, classroom with tables pushed to the perimeter, stage, empty cafeteria, or gym can work.

Lesson Progression

1. Tape the ladder structures prior to the lesson.

2. Ask students to explore and then talk about what they noticed about the structure.

3. Give students the challenge to "find center" and then stand back to observe the physical problem solving and sense making.

4. Pause the action when two or more groups have found an answer to talk and show the rest of the class how and what they did to find their solution.

5. Provide time for written and visual reflection.

Extending the Learning

Provide one or more of the following challenges to extend the learning.

- *How many different places/contexts/ways can you find half, middle, or center?*

- *Investigate even and odd numbers using the ladder structure. Using sticky notes numbered 1 through 25, label each cell of the ladder. Investigate these questions: What number is in the middle of 5 and 9? 2 and 8? 1 and 4?*

- *Fold some paper in half. How many ways can you find half? Can you find the center? Does your method work with different shapes of paper: Square? Rectangular? Triangular?*

▶ **Figure 3.14**

Lesson Background

This lesson was inspired by a game called "My Turn, Your Turn," which I found in *Mathematics Their Way* (Baratta-Lorton 1995), a comprehensive progression of hands-on, materials-based, whole-body K–2 math learning and teaching from the 1970s. The book described the game briefly and showed an image of children walking on top of a long, low bench that had been partitioned into sections using tape. What sparked my curiosity was a comment by the author that, prior to playing the game, the children should work together to find the center of the long, oblong space and take as much time as they needed to do this. I wondered what would happen if I re-created the structure with tape on the floor and simply asked the children to "find the center" without any elaboration., see Figure 3.14.

Opening the Lesson

I opened this lesson by telling the class: "Each group will spend some time getting to know their taped structure. When you're done taking a close look, we'll gather back here and have a conversation about what you noticed." It's important for children to first make sense of the structure or materials you are asking them to use. They will do this by using their eyes and gestures (pointing and so on), and they will also use their whole bodies, sometimes vigorously. This physical exploration may look random, but watch closely and you will see them employ a great amount of body focus in making sense of the ladder structure. The students' physical exploration included all of the following actions:

▶ **Figure 3.15**

- running down the outside of the ladder on the left and then back on the right, then hopping on one foot, stepping a little, and hopping back
- moving along the ladder by stepping randomly or by making sure to step in each space
- crawling on hands and knees and bear crawls (hands and feet)
- sidestepping others (See Figure 3.15.)
- one-footed hopping over two spaces or stepping over two spaces
- running in place, jumping a little, down and up, and hopscotching (hopping on one foot in the center of a space, then landing with two feet on either side of the next space)
- jumping and hopping, walking backward, tiptoeing
- placing two feet inside one space and then putting two feet on the outside lines, split apart
- running and sliding

These explorations showed me that students were making sense of the scale of the object, which was at least six times longer than they were. Their rhythmic and intentional stepping and hopping highlighted how they were recognizing and making sense of the ladder's regular and repeated progression of cells.

Noticing and Making Sense of Structure

At some point an activity like this may appear more hyper than it was before, and that's a good time to have everyone sit down and have a chat about what they noticed about the ladder. These moments are important because they not only offer a break in the action but also support students in focusing on the salient details for solving the upcoming challenge. Their noticings also help you, as the teacher, get a better idea of how they are working to make sense of the structure. In this case, the students connected the structure itself to an object with which they were already familiar ("It looks like a jungle gym." "It looks like a front porch." "It could be a math tool if there was a 1, 2, 3, 4, 5 on it to 25. It could be like a math line maybe?" "It's sort of like a ladder that you can't pick up."). They also noticed the repetition and regularity of the structure ("It looks like hopscotch." "It sorta looks like a pattern thing. If you jump a specific way, like one foot, one foot, two feet . . ."). They also noticed the physical properties ("It's blue." "It's rough.").

My next move was to get the challenge started and, at the same time, make it clear I expected students to be in control of their bodies. "OK, now it's time for your challenge. I want you to work with your group to find the center. As you move your bodies, I want to see that you are in control of your movements. You're probably also going to need to talk about your ideas with each other, so you will need to make sure to listen to each other and take turns talking."

Working to Prove What You Think You Know

One group (Abel, Alina, Oscar, Louis, and Jaelyn) started with two people deciding independently to start at each end of the ladder and count toward the middle. This created some chaos and a traffic jam of sorts. In response, Abel took the lead and orchestrated a more organized effort by making sure the pathways from each end were free of obstacles (e.g., other kids). He was focused on the discrepancies in one-to-one orchestrated stepping in each individual cell of the ladder. To rectify the imprecise stepping on the part of the children acting as counters, he assiduously interviewed the others in his group with a very earnest query: "Are you a fast counter or a slow counter?" followed by "OK . . . Oscar. Go back to the start." Oscar and Alina started again from each end, carefully stepping in each box, but not in sync with each other.

Oscar ended in a box, saying, "This is twelve." This still did not resolve anything because it turned out that Alina got eleven. They tried again by positioning another group member in what they though was the center, which was a different location from the first one they identified and was basically determined by educated guess. The one-to-one stepping efforts and the debates continued for a while longer, and then I stepped in.

> **Me:** *Did you guys figure something out?*
>
> **Louis:** *We figured this was it* [pointing to the location they had determined was the center].
>
> **Me:** *I'm not sure I understand where it is. Can you show me with your body?*
>
> **Abel:** [Standing in the spot] *We were walking with two fast counters and two slow counters. Some stood right where the center is . . .*

Me: *But there are three of you in a row. Which one of you is in the center?* [To Abel] *Are you there? So how are you going to check?*

Abel: *By counting, by make suring it's equal on each side* [gesturing with his arms in both directions, toward each end of the ladder]. [Giving more directions to his group] *How 'bout you two go there* [to each end] *and slow walkers count each beat.*

Me: [Noticing more kids on the tape] *How many people do we need on the tape right now?*

Abel: *One in the middle and two going toward the sides. If we find that if both of you found the same numbers, it'll be the middle. OK . . . go!*

The kids counted together, but once again one ended on eleven and the other on twelve. They tried again, finding eleven and thirteen. At this point I decided to pause the conversation for a minute because their physical reasoning was not helping them gain ground.

Me: *So I have a question for you guys: How many total spaces are there in the path?*

Louis: *I counted twenty-five.*

Me: *Are you counting spaces or pieces of tape?*

Louis: *Spaces.*

Me: *Does this group agree that there are twenty-five spaces?*

All: *Yes!*

Thinking they could benefit from the perspective of watching and listening to the reasoning and explanation of another group, I invited them to sit and watch another group (including Kyle, Hugo, Sara, and Laia) share their process.

Kyle: *So one of us did what we thought was the middle, and how we checked, because we measured how many squares on either side. And then the same being on each side would be the middle. And if it wasn't, we tried a different square to see if that was the middle.*

Me: *So can you show us what you did to figure it out?*

Hugo: *I standed right here and then Sara went down . . .*

Me: *How did you decide on the space where Sara is?*

Hugo: *The first time we did it, Sara didn't get the same amount, so she moved down one and then we got the same amount on each side.*

Me: *So you made a guess about where the middle was and then you did . . . what?*

Laia: *Counted the boxes on each side.*

Me: *That's sort of like what Group 1 did, too. Group 1, what do you guys think?*

Jaelyn (who had stepped back from the action during the problem solving and was now sitting down on her group's structure, facing the other team): *I think* this *is the center because we could all even up with the middle of theirs.*

Me: *Oh, interesting. Does Group 2 want to try to check this and see if this really is the center? Jaelyn decided that's where the center is because she's looking at where Sara is right now. Does Group 2 want to check?* [They count thirteen on one side and eleven on the other.]

Me: *Oh, that's the reverse of your count last time, which was eleven on one side and thirteen on the other side. . . . So what does that mean you need to do now to find the middle?*

It turns out that Sara was not actually in the identified center of Group 2's structure. She moved into that spot and both groups were now "evened up."

This challenge motivated students to pay close attention to and harness the salient details of the ladder structure in their problem solving. Proving that they had the right answer required them to make use of three novel tools: their own bodies, one-to-one correspondence, and the structure itself. The ladder was too big to easily identify its middle; as a result, multiple moving bodies had to be employed in very precise ways to verify the location of center.

COLLABORATIVE ROPE POLYGONS

(45–60 minutes; grades 3–6)

In this activity, students work collaboratively to investigate and construct regular polygons with their bodies and a twelve-foot length of clothesline rope. This process requires close thinking about the salient properties of regular polygons, including vertices and angles, and requires students to engage and, ultimately, adapt their lived experience and prior knowledge of polygons, measurement, angles, regular intervals, and repeated reasoning while attending to the challenge. No matter the grade level, you can use this activity to both assess students' current geometric knowledge and move them forward toward new insights and understanding. It can be extended to irregular polygons and convex angles in fifth and sixth grades. The investigation takes about forty-five to sixty minutes, and you'll need follow-up sessions for recording and analyzing the data the students collect.

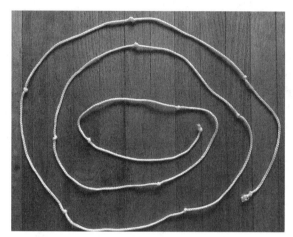

▶ **Figure 3.16**

Math: Measuring; reasoning with shapes and their attributes; connecting geometric forms with number concepts; drawing, identifying, and describing lines, angles, and other geometrical figures; classifying shapes by properties of their lines and angles; composing polygons

Materials: One twelve-foot piece of nylon clothesline per group of four or five students, knotted thirteen times to create twelve one-foot segments (see Figure 3.16).

Space: Enough room for two to six groups of four or five to spread out enough to explore the dimensions of the twelve-foot rope. An LGI room, a cafeteria, a gym, a stage, a cleared-out classroom, an outdoor space, or your own classroom with desks and chairs pushed to the perimeter of the room should work. If you choose to do the activity outside, wait until you are back inside to have conversations about and debrief the activity.

Lesson Progression

1. Ask students in their teams to investigate their knotted rope. After one or two minutes, reconvene the class to share noticings and wonderings about this new mathematical tool.

2. Challenge teams to create one or more regular polygons using their bodies and the rope.

3. Observe and engage groups in conversations about their efforts. Conversations can be initiated out of both curiosity and need, but it is also amazing to just stand back, listen in, and watch what they can do by themselves. I often jump in at the exact moment a group has figured a way out of a stuck place by themselves. When in doubt, wait another minute and then decide whether a particular group needs you to intervene.

4. Pause the action when each group has created at least one polygon to facilitate a class conversation about what students are noticing about the process.

5. Send students back to work with a specific challenge related to the insights, misconceptions, or challenges revealed during the discussion.

6. Close the lesson with a final conversation and a chance for students to make notes of what they created with the rope. These notes can be utilized in a separate session to investigate and connect the moving math to more formal visual and numeric reasoning.

Extending the Learning

This activity has good potential for further discussions and extension activities on organizing data; investigating the relationship between factors and the perimeter and area of regular polygons; the nature of polygons (regular or irregular, convex or concave); development and application of geometric vocabulary; and written reflection on mathematical activity and problem solving. You can also repeat the activity with further questions to explore. You can also pose these questions, developed by The Math Forum at NCTM's Max Ray-Riek, as additional challenges to groups that seem to be done and are waiting for their classmates to finish up:

- How can you convince me you have found all the possible shapes?
- What shapes did you find easily? Were there any you struggled to find?
- How many different squares can be made? How many different rhombi?
- Can you make more than one triangle that fits the rules?
- Can you make more than one hexagon that fits the rules?
- Can you make more than one dodecagon that fits the rules?

Lesson Background

I first came across the idea of using ropes to make polygons while I was reading Dr. Jasmine Ma's dissertation to learn more about the work she does investigating whole-body math learning with middle school, high school, and college students. I wanted to create a similar activity for elementary students and found a problem online that said it was about "making geometric shapes outside with ropes," but the text itself actually prompted students to model the activity using yarn at their desks. I knew that the necessary precision would be difficult to attain that way. So, with the help of some colleagues, I devised the following challenge:

> Using your rope and your bodies, your challenge is to make one or more regular/equilateral polygons with your group.

This activity is highly adaptable and an intriguing challenge with just enough information to get students started. And, in my experience, it sparks students' curiosity rather than walking them down a well-marked path. You may want to focus on the idea of regular polygons, as I did with the third and fourth graders discussed here, or you can challenge your fifth and sixth graders to focus on equilateral shapes, which has the potential to lead to exploration of concave polygons. When you ask kids to work collaboratively and use their bodies to create as many regular rope polygons as they can, the medium itself creates challenges that require specific and precise body- and language-based communication to negotiate the collaborative construction of the polygons.

Opening and Tracking the Lesson

I opened the lesson by giving students a new tool (the rope) for thinking mathematically and asking them to investigate the material. After a few minutes, I asked them what they noticed. Just like in the "Proving Center" activity, making sense of the material is the first step in making sense of the activity itself. Some groups will notice the knots right away and set out to figure out the measurement of the intervals without prompting, in which case you can provide them with the challenge. Other groups might miss this detail altogether, and you can decide whether or not to be explicit about this piece of information when you are giving them the challenge.

The third graders I worked with had explored the rope quite vigorously and without focus and they had not noticed the relevant properties of the rope. To address both issues, I said, "Here's what I'd like you to do now. This activity needs to be about conversation between you and the others in your group. Your challenge is to make a shape out of this rope. And there's a special way we're going to do it. This rope has knots in it, as you've noticed. So the space between the knots measures out one foot in length. Each distance between the knots is the same. So, I'm wondering if you, in your groups, can use this rope to make one shape that has equal sides. Remember, all members of your group need to be involved with making the shape using your bodies. Decide with your group what shape you want to make."

Third Graders Work to Measure Out a Square

For one particular group of third graders, this challenge centered around issues of measurement. Ella said, "I have an idea. . . . Guys, just wait!" Maddison and Naomi were on each end of the rope, and Blake was in the middle, holding the rope too. Ella gestured in both directions to get them

▶ **Figure 3.17** Third graders work to make a square with the rope.

▶ **Figure 3.18** Third graders and their hard-won square!

to stop. "I have an idea to make it equal. You see there's knots? Maybe these knots could help us make different lengths. Like with the sides."

Naomi then took the lead and encouraged each student in the group to grab two knots, with one knot between them (so each would be holding two one-foot intervals). After several failed attempts and a lot of standing up and sitting down, Naomi led the group in positioning the rope on the floor with parallel edges that were two feet and four feet long.

Then Blake said, "We have to make a *square*. That's not a square." Naomi gestured and touched the rope where Maddison and Blake should hold it, and suddenly they formed a square (See Figures 3.17 and 3.18).

I had been moving between groups, but at this point I could tell it was almost time to pause the whole class and check in. Before doing so, I asked this group: "How can we check that it's a square?"

Maddison counted, "One, two, three, four," and pointed to each knot on each edge.

Blake had a different approach. He counted out loud, "One, two, one, two, one, two. . . . It's the 'one knot, two knots' pattern."

Wanting to make sure I understood, I asked, "So you're counting these knots as a way to tell if it's a square? Maddison, tell me what you're counting, because they're counting ones and twos and you're counting fours."

Naomi replied for Maddison: "She's counting the corners."

It turned out that Maddison was counting a corner knot, the two knots partitioning each edge into three segments, and the corner knot at the next vertex. Contrast this with the "one, two, one, two" pattern employed by the rest of the group, in which each vertex was a "one" and there were two knots visible on each side of the square, creating three one-foot intervals. Despite the difference, it was striking to me that everyone in this group saw the knots as the thing to measure, not the intervals of rope between the knots, confirming that children need repeated exposure to measurement in diverse contexts to fully harness it as a useful mathematical tool.

Whole-Group Discussion: Comparing Experiences

When I got the whole class back together, I asked, "What did you notice while you were working to make a shape?" It was clear that, despite the disorganization of their initial exploration of the material, they had all interacted with the rope in ways that had changed their perspective on the tool and that measurement had been a major focus of their conversations.

Gabriel (from another group): *It's hard to make corners.*

Me: *Can you say more?*

Gabriel: *Like with the knots, they won't bend into a corner shape, so it's kinda hard to make the corners.*

Naomi: *It's hard to make things even.*

Me: *Can you say more?*

Naomi: *So, our team was trying to make a square, but first we made a rectangle, a really messed-up rectangle. The two ends kept on falling apart and then we let Ella do it, and she made it go really easy.*

Me: *What did Ella do that made making the shape easier?*

Naomi: *She held each one, like she put them together but holding each one separately.*

Gabriel: *You have to divide twelve into four, which is three. Then we had an even square because there was three feet on each side.*

Me: *How did you know it was three feet?*

Gabriel: *I counted each foot. I didn't count the knots because there's eleven knots, but there's twelve feet of rope.* [There were actually thirteen knots and twelve feet of rope, but I think knots at the ends of their rope had come undone.]

Since Ella and Naomi's group had also made a square, I knew that a physical and verbal explanation from Gabriel's group might help them gain some perspective on their efforts. Gabriel's group asked if they could show their work and stood up with their rope.

Gabriel: *I'm pretty sure all of us knew that twelve divided by four equals three, so we did "one foot, two foot, three foot"* [running his hands down the length of each interval as he counts], *so we made sure we had two knots and three feet* [of rope].

Me: *I want to point out what I think you're seeing. Group 1 told me that when they were thinking about how they knew the sides were going to be equal, they counted two knots and saw if it matched the other sides. And then there are the corner knots, and Maddison said, "I know that it's a square because it's got four knots on this side," and that is how she described it was a square. Now I want to hear what this group sees as equal sides.*

Gabriel: *We saw equal sides on this because of the double knots and we also noticed that there were three spaces in between the knots. It was three feet because in between each knot was one foot and then* [he counts on] *two feet, three feet on each side.*

Fourth Graders: When Previously Unnoticed Properties Become Apparent

A fourth-grade group I worked with had much more prior knowledge of polygons and their properties and, in contrast with the third-grade group, quickly figured out the measurement aspect. (See Figures 3.19–3.21) However, they were well challenged with the task of constructing shapes in

▶ **Figure 3.19** Fourth graders record the different polygons they created during their session.

▶ **Figure 3.20** Fourth graders in the initial stages of figuring out how to work with the knotted rope.

▶ **Figure 3.21** These fourth graders have figured out how three people (and six hands) can work together to create a hexagon.

this new context. After they had created one or two polygons, I sat everyone down and asked: "What were some of the things you noticed while you were making your polygons with your group?" Their answers showed me that the rope itself had forced students to pay attention to and struggle with aspects of polygons that had previously gone unnoticed.

Christina: *We made a pentagon, and we didn't use all of the rope; because a few people on the sides were dropping them off.*

Maria: *We made a square that was three by three.*

Me: *And did you end up doing another shape too?*

Maria: *Yeah, we did a triangle.*

Me: *What did you notice about making the shapes?*

Sophia: *You had to hold the rope taut or it didn't really look like what it was supposed to be.*

Luke: *Sometimes when you try to make one shape, you made another shape that you didn't realize.*

Me: *Can you give us some details about what you mean?*

Luke: *Well, we were trying to make a hexagon. Then we ended up making like a triangle.*

Me: *And how did that happen?*

Luke: *Someone let go of the corner, and someone grabbed the corner, and everything went weird and it was a triangle.*

Me: *So, I have a question. How many people did you have in your group?*

Luke: *Four.*

Me: *If you're trying to make a hexagon, how many corners, how many angles is that going to have?*

John: *Six.*

Me: *It's going to have six, but you only have four people, so how did you manage that?*

Luke: *I don't know.*

Me: *Does anyone in his group want to say how that worked?*

Nathan (from a different group): *Well, we made a rectangle, but we only had three people, so I grabbed two of the corners.*

Me: *So if there's only three people, how many hands do they have?*

Multiple kids voices: *Six.*

I left that idea to hang out in the collective consciousness and sent the groups back to work for a little while longer. This was a fascinating moment. Although in our initial conversations at the beginning of the lesson, these students very clearly thought they had mastered polygons, on the whole most groups were convinced that they could make a shape only if they had the same number of people as vertices. I let the kids get back to work and started hearing conversations that indicated that they were making more use of both their bodies and the rope in the construction of the regular polygons. The conversation from a group working to make a triangle sounded like this:

Ben: *It'd be four on each side.*

Meghan: *No, it'd be three on each side.*

Ben: *Nope.*

Joselyn: *It'd be four on each side. Look. A triangle has three sides and so in order to add up to twelve, you'd have to have four, four, and four, which makes twelve. If you had three, three, and three, that would make nine.*

Meghan: *Ooh yeah.*

Another group with three members was working on a hexagon. They seemed to have solved the number-of-bodies-versus-number-of-hands issue but were struggling with how to close the figure. This challenge arose because the rope had thirteen knots. When you make a hexagon, there are six vertices, which require six hands, but in this three-person group there was one knot left and they were debating about what to do next. One girl told me they needed to hold together the ends of the rope.

When we reconvened one last time I could tell that the children had made sense of the rope as a construction tool:

Me: *First of all, let's share out what polygons each group made.*

[Students reported that they had made a triangle, a rectangle, a hexagon, a dodecagon, and an octagon.]

Me: *How many edges did the octagon have?*

Nora: *Eight.*

Me: *And how long were those sides?*

Nora: *They went in a pattern: two, one, two, one, two, one, two, one.*

Me: *So was it a regular polygon? What do you guys think I mean when I say "regular"?*

A few kids at the same time: *A shape with equal sides and equal angles!*

Kira: *All its sides are even. It's a square but a different shape.*

Me: *So if they made an octagon, and its sides were two and one, were all of those sides equal?*

Kira: *No.*

Figures 3.22 through 3.24 show the work students did to record their work directly after the activity itself by recording the polygons their groups created. The next day they also created tables that explored the relationships between regular polygons and the factors at play in each shape's perimeter. In particular, notice the strategy by which the children recorded their polygons.

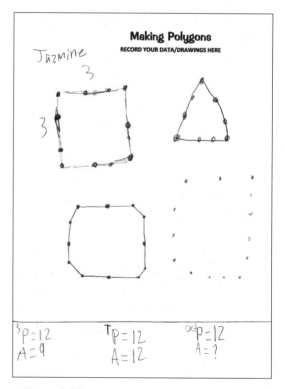

▶ **Figure 3.22**

Although this was an open-ended prompt to "record your shapes" and no direction was given to the children about how to do this, their work illustrates their awareness of the number of vertices in each possible polygon.

This activity created a potent environment in which to challenge students' current understanding of polygons by requiring verbal and body-based specificity and precision. Students needed to apply their prior knowledge of measurement, factors, and geometry to create their shapes. Creating any chosen polygon relied on how each member of the group positioned and stabilized the rope, which created many opportunities for reasoning with peers about the math in question.

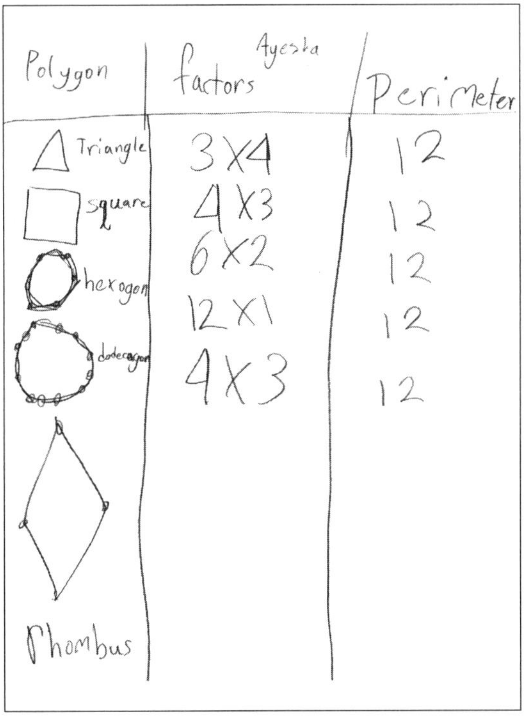

▶ **Figure 3.23**

▶ **Figure 3.24**

The next four chapters focus on pairing the whole, moving body with mathematical ideas and concepts in a dance-making setting. Chapters 4 and 5 lay out the lesson progression and details of Math in Your Feet for intermediate students; Chapter 6 addresses the methods with which teachers can facilitate such a venture; and Chapter 7 provides an adaptation of the Math in Your Feet work for the primary grades.

Chapter Four

Math in Your Feet, Part 1
Understand, Experiment, and Create

I n this chapter I focus on the first three stages of the Math in Your Feet lesson progression for grades 3–6, which can also be adjusted for second graders in the second half of the school year. The final three stages can be found in Chapter 5 and a description of the K–2 version of this work is in Chapter 7.

Math in Your Feet: An Overview

For intermediate students, Math in Your Feet is organized around a six-stage process (though two stages are intertwined) through which students create and transform an eight-beat pattern with a partner using both dance and math ideas at the same time. The ladder chart in Figure 4.1 shows these six stages.

Stage 1: Understand

In the first stage, you lay out the challenge for students to make their own math-and-dance pattern. You can do this by watching some recommended videos of percussive dance (see the Appendix) and briefly reviewing the ladder chart (Figure 4.1) with your students. This chart becomes the road map for the entire process. Students also need to understand the challenge ahead. You will orient students to their dance spaces and have them experiment with the directions, movements, and foot positions they can use to create their patterns. This first stage usually takes forty-five to sixty minutes.

Stages 2 and 3: Experiment and Create

In the next two intertwined, cyclical stages, students create two different four-beat patterns (called pattern A and pattern B), with the goal of making the two patterns as different as possible. You will observe and assist the teams as they get started and work on pattern A, pausing the action from time to time to bring up demonstration teams, talk about the work as a group, and introduce the idea of *sameness* in the dancing. The same process applies to pattern B, but this time you will focus on the idea of *difference*. These two stages usually take forty-five to sixty minutes each.

Stage 4: Combine

In the fourth stage, students work to combine their two patterns to create a new, eight-beat pattern, called pattern C. Students can combine their patterns in any of four ways—AB, BA, AA, or BB—but the real challenge for physical and spatial cognition as well as mathematical thinking lies in deciding how to handle the transition between beat 4 (where the first pattern ends) and beat 5 (where the second pattern begins). This stage usually takes forty-five to sixty minutes.

Stage 5: Transform

In this stage, students transform their patterns using reflection symmetry. This includes a teacher-led lesson, independent group work, discussion, and some games to help students make sense of the transformation process. You can do this in one sixty-minute session or in two thirty- to forty-five-minute sessions. I've found that saving the games for a second session helps overall student comprehension.

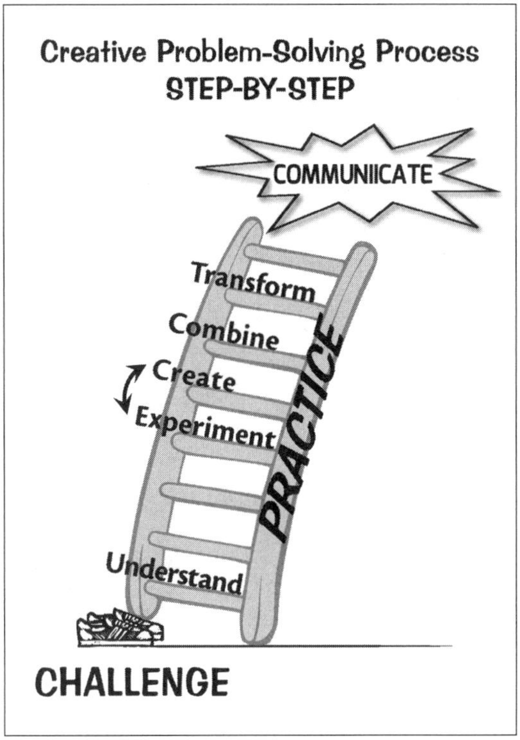

▶ **Figure 4.1** The six-stage process for Math in Your Feet

Stage 6: Communicate

There are several possibilities for a final dance presentation, which I discuss in Chapter 5. Students should also be supported to express their math ideas and reflect on the process of making math and dance verbally and in written and mapped form as a way to formalize their understanding of the embedded mathematics. The opportunities for children to communicate and reflect upon their work are also the tools with which you will assess their work and learning. I address all of this in detail in Chapter 8.

As long as you follow the *progression* of the math-and-dance-making process, the other aspects are fairly flexible. For example, it's easy to pause the action at any point and start up again at another time from where you left off. You can work through the activity progression in ten-minute chunks (although realistically your students may balk at this and request longer sessions) or you can decide to focus on it using a more standard forty-five- to sixty-minute lesson length. Let's get started!

Planning

If this is your first time leading dance-based learning, please consider finding support in a colleague or other adult as you begin this exciting journey! If you are a school-based educator, both music and physical education specialists have a wealth of knowledge about organizing moving bodies and could become excellent resources and collaborators. Please also know you do not need to do the entire progression of lessons the first time you try it. You can decide how far down the math-and-dance-making path you want to go. Whatever you do will be beneficial for your students, socially, physically, and cognitively. Find a low-key, low-stakes context like the end of the school year or before a break to get your feet wet; even just leading students through the process of making a pattern A is a great first step. Embrace this as an adventure and ask your students to join you! Inviting them to learn with you is a potentially powerful and inspiring experience for everyone. Not only is including your students as partners in exploring something new a great life lesson for them, but it might also help soothe any doubts or jitters you have about getting everyone up and moving. This will be a fun, useful, and invigorating experience for both you and your students. To make sure things go as smoothly as possible, here are some things to put in place before you get started.

Choose Your Work Space

The math-and-dance work is inherently playful, but holding class outside on the playground should be the absolute last choice. It has all sorts of distractions: heat, cold, bugs, planes flying overhead, and other kids playing and making noise. The outdoors is also not at all the right place for giving detailed instructions and having focused conversations with a group of students, activities that make up at least half of the math-and-dance work and lessons. For similar reasons, a hallway is also not an appropriate option. Instead, consider the following options first:

- The best-case scenario is an open space free of chairs and desks, such as a stage, a gym, a cafeteria, a music room, a large-group instruction room, or an unused classroom. This will allow you to leave the taped squares down for the course of your math-and-dance unit even while others are using the space at other times of day.

- You can also do this work in most classrooms. Have your students push their chairs under their desks and then have them tape down the dance spaces in the spots where the chairs usually are when they're pulled out. Or, you can push the desks to the perimeter of the room and build the squares in the middle. When you're done moving for the day, you can move the desks back on top of the squares.

Make the Dance Spaces

The dance spaces are made with blue low-tack painters tape, found at most hardware and big-box stores. There have been only two times in my entire teaching career when the painters tape did not come off cleanly. One was on weird fifty-year-old tiles in a university building in Saskatchewan. The other was when it was placed on carpet, but the kids had poked a million holes in the tape with their pencils, which made it almost impossible to pull it off the floor. Do *not* use duct tape or regular masking tape on carpets or tiles. An alternative to painters tape is the tape made specifically for gym floors. Your PE teacher will know how to order it (one option is www.gophersport.com/pe/teacher-resources-cones-markers/deluxe-vinyl-floor-tape). This is my second choice because it's very stretchy, which makes it hard to measure and cut accurately, unless you've got square-foot tiles in your room (which basically do the measuring for you). It also doesn't stick to carpet very well.

Once you've got your tape, it's time to make the squares!

- Each square is two feet by two feet. Premeasuring and cutting the tape first helps make the process of making the spaces literally square much easier. Measure and cut (or tear) first, and then construct.

- Squares should be in pairs, with approximately three inches between the two squares in each pair. Ideally, there should be six to twelve inches between the pairs of boxes, but do what you need to do to make it work for your space.

- If you have room, construct a set of demonstration boxes in a location in the "front" of your space. Or, students can demonstrate their work in their own squares and the rest of the students can turn their bodies to watch, as necessary.

- Consider having students construct their own dance spaces. This adds a little extra time to the whole process, but for the most part, the benefits of experiencing and creating *squareness* at a new scale off the page is a fantastic way to deepen your students' experience and create new understanding of this seemingly familiar shape.

Gather the Materials

In addition to tape, you will need the following items:

- a *laptop and projector* or other technology with which to view online videos

- a few preselected *videos* that show a variety of percussive dance forms in action (see suggestions in the Appendix)

- *classroom posters* for students to refer to (see Web Link 4.1)

- *word study and reflection prompts* (see Chapter 8)

A Note About Modeling Language

Throughout the rest of the chapter, I provide at various points a script of sorts that models the tone and content of the kinds of conversations I have with students at different stages during the math-and-dance-making process. These scripts are not meant to be followed exactly; along with the videos, this approximation of my classroom voice will give you a sense of how the lessons and activities are introduced, paced, and sequenced.

Web Link 4.1

A PDF of classroom posters for the Math in Your Feet work is provided at

http://hein.pub/mathmres4.1

Stage 1: Understand— Introducing the Math-and-Dance-Making Process

The first step in the math-and-dance making is to provide students with the big picture regarding the project and its stages. This includes a brief introduction to percussive dance and introducing the route you will take, the goal of making original math-and-dance patterns, and an orientation to the movement variables.

INTRODUCING THE WORK AHEAD

(15 minutes)

> *Goal:* Provide an overview of the dance styles on which this work is based. Provide an overview of the activities in this program.

Key Points

A big-picture overview brings purpose to these first introductory steps. To start, show a few videos of percussive dance (suggestions are listed in the Appendix) to pique your students' interest. Then introduce students to the ladder graphic. Here's an example of what I say to kids:

> *I'm going to give you a challenge! You're going to make up your own percussive dance pattern. The process of making your own dance is called* choreography. *Let's say that word together slowly . . . . A choreographer is a problem solver, just like in math—you have a question and you work to find an answer. This chart* [the ladder] *illustrates the steps we will take as we create our dance patterns. As you can see, it will take more than one session to create our math-and-dance patterns. The first step is to* understand *the challenge. So, everything we do right now will help us understand how to solve this challenge that I am giving you. Let's get started!*

The ladder chart provides students with a quick overview of how each step of the process follows the one before and where they are in the process at any given moment.

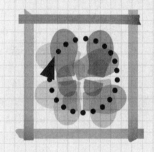

Try It Yourself!

You do not need to dance or move in front of your class, but you should at least review the inventory of movements before you bring it to your students. It will also be very useful for you to try out the movements by yourself at some point. Asking kids to demonstrate for the class a certain movement or combination of moves, like turns, is more than acceptable, but it will be beneficial for you to have a feel for what it means to move around in the square using different kinds of movements, directions, and foot positions.

ORIENTING STUDENTS TO DANCE SPACES

(10–15 minutes)

Goal: Orient students to their dance spaces and introduce expectations for a safe classroom focused on moving and making, including an emphasis on working together and staying within the confines of their squares.

Math focus: Spatial and geometric concepts; spatial orientation; attending to precision.

Key Points

For students to get the most out of the math-and-dance making, they need to be explicitly introduced and oriented to the small and seemingly straight-forward dance space. This activity helps familiarize students with their new dance spaces and, ultimately, helps them think and move precisely. This is also probably the only time you will be giving specific, step-by-step instructions to the students as you walk them through the different movement variables. Because most of your time will be spent as a facilitator and an observer, it may be helpful to remind them that after this segment, they will be in charge of everything they do in their own squares. I recommend try-ing out the following progression of instructions before you lead students through it.

Students choose (or are assigned) partners. If you have an odd number of students, a team of three will work fine. Students should, if at all possible, keep the same teammate throughout the math-and-dance-making process. To start, students sit in their individual dance spaces, *side by side with both partners facing the same direction.* Students should create and perform their math-and-dance patterns while standing side by side in their squares or otherwise facing the same direction. This allows teammates to identify more easily whether they are using the same rights and lefts in their foot-work. Since many of the conversations about this work are about sameness and change, this orientation should be consistent throughout the process.

The following illustrates how I might lead students through exploring and experimenting with the different movement variables.

These squares are your home base. This is where all your work will take place. While you're working, you need to stay inside your squares.

Now let's get oriented to these spaces. I'm going to be giving a lot of directions so you'll need to listen carefully. First, stand up in the middle of your dance space. Where you are standing is called "center." Let's say that together. If you look up at this chart [of movement variables; see Figure 2.5], you'll see that "Center" is listed with other options in the "Direction" category.

Introducing and reinforcing the idea of sameness starts right at the very beginning. At this early stage, reminding students to do the same thing as their partner helps them pay closer attention to what both they and their partner are doing. Later, once they have become more familiar with the inventory of options that build the dance patterns, you will more explicitly connect the idea of unison (dancing the same) to the parallel idea of congruence created when all relevant properties of the math-and-dance pattern are danced the same.

You and your teammate must work together to make sure you are both doing the same things. Take your right foot and point it to the front of your square. Now take your right foot and point it to the back of your square. Make sure that you and your teammate are both doing the same thing; *if one of you is touching the tape but the other has your foot outside the space, you are not doing the same thing, so you'll both need to keep your feet inside the tape.*

Now take your right foot and point it to the right side. Feet together. Great! Take your left foot and point it to the left side. Fantastic.

OK, let's look at the "Movement Variables" chart and see if we can figure out the one direction we have not yet used in this activity. That's right: diagonal. Where are the diagonals in our squares? How many can you find? Work with your partner to figure this out. You've got one minute.

Diagonals can be found by splitting the feet apart between a front corner and a back corner. They can also be the direction of an individual foot, as in "Step in the upper right corner."

UNDERSTANDING THE CHALLENGE

(15–20 minutes)

Goal: Give students the necessary information and experience to start making up their own math-and-dance patterns.

Math focus: Unitizing and creating a pattern unit (four beats); *constructing* patterns; analyzing pattern properties; combining movement variables; working with spatial and geometric concepts.

(specifically, understanding and combining turns using a unit turn of one-fourth, or ninety degrees—you can choose to use the terminology *one-fourth* (or *one-quarter*) *turn* or *ninety-degree turn* depending on the needs of your students).

Key Points

Now that students have a sense of *where* they can move in their squares, they need to know *how* they can move into those places and in what positions their feet might land.

> *Let's look at the ladder chart again. We've already worked to understand the different directions in which we can move in our dance spaces. Today we're going to look at the other things we need to understand before we can experiment with the movement variables and start making up our own dance steps. First of all, your pattern will be four beats long. Let's snap out four steady beats together—one, two, three, four. Great. On each beat, our feet will hit the ground somewhere inside the square.*

Emphasizing a four-beat pattern will help clarify the idea of pattern unit in this new dance context.

> *Let's start by experimenting with the movement* jump *and some different directions we can use while we jump. What direction do you want to jump in? We'll start with our feet together in center. Do two jumps—on the first beat forward* [or whichever direction your class has chosen] *and on the second beat into center, like "Forward, center." Say those with me while we try it: "Forward, center."*

Students can give you suggestions for different directions and you can direct the whole group, for example: "Ready, go: right side, center. OK, try that again. Ready, go: right side, center. Let's do that again. Say the words with me while you move." You can give them a minute to experiment with their partners to find how many directions in their squares they can jump to with feet together and then back to center.

Next, do a similar demonstration and exploration around jumps and the different directions in which students can split their feet. Feet can be split to the side; with one foot front and one foot back; to the front right or left diagonal (which means left foot in the front left corner and right foot in the back right corner); with two feet in the front corners; or with two feet in the back corners. Give students time to experiment and then move to the third movement variable:

Now I'm wondering if jumping is the only movement option. What other options do you see under the "Movement" category? Let's try a step. Who wants to show me what it would look like to step to the front of our square? Great! Let's all put our feet together in center. Then we'll take two steps forward to the front and then two steps back to center. We'll use the direction words "forward, forward, center, center."

I then have students try stepping to the diagonals and the sides of the square before introducing the slide.

Who wants to show me a step with one foot and then sliding the other foot to meet it? Let's all try it. Step, slide. So that move is two beats, "step, slide." You can also slide back with two feet together. Try that out with your partner.

    Now let's try out a touch. A touch is where your foot touches the floor but you don't stand on it, like when you take a step. With your partner, experiment with all the different directions you can touch your toe or your heel in your square.

Introducing Turns

There is one movement we have not yet done. Can anyone tell me what it is? That's right! A turn! Let's look at the "Turns" chart on the wall. When we turn in our squares, we can turn to four different sides. Let's turn to the first of four sides. How far is that in fractions? That's right; it's one-fourth of the way around. Let's try a jump with our feet together that includes turning to the first of the four sides of our square. Let's turn to the right. Which direction will you face when you're done? Toward the clock or toward the windows? [Or whatever is on the target wall and the opposite wall.] Make sure you and your partner are turning in the same direction. This turn has a measurement of ninety degrees.

    Now jump and turn one-fourth to your left to get back to where you started! Everyone should be facing the front again.

The whole class should try four one-fourth turns to the left, all together on your count. If you are working with students who do not yet know the measurement of right angles, it is up to you how to proceed. You can use the fractional term (quarter turn), but I have found that third graders are able understand the idea of ninety-degree turns easily after relating it to the four sides of the square or the four walls in a room. This will give third graders a valuable and visceral experience with this concept for future explorations in fourth grade and beyond.

You can also experiment with combinations of directions for the turns, for example: left, right, right, left. If you have decided to focus on the degrees of turns with your class, this next question will set the stage for connecting the fractional measurement with the rotations:

> *If you are turning to face a new side and that turn is one-fourth of the way around, how far is that in degrees?*

If you opt to stay with fractional measurements, then continue to use the terminology of fractions and the number of sides of the square throughout the rest of the math-and-dance-making process, including your discussions of turns.

> *How far will you go if you turn from facing front to facing back, all in one beat? That's right: halfway. How many 90s is that? How many sides? That's two 90s, or sides, in one beat, which makes it a turn of one-half, or 180 degrees. Let's all try a 180-degree turn to the left. Which way will you be facing if you do a 180-degree turn in one beat?*
>
> *OK, let's all sit down. Who wants to show me a three-fourths turn? How many degrees will she be turning if she turns to the third side? How many nineties is that in one beat?*

If a student (or the class) has trouble figuring out where to end up, have the students turn slowly without a jump, counting the sides they pass as they go—first side, one ninety; second side, two nineties; third side, three nineties.

Final Words Before Starting Work on Pattern A

There are only three explicit rules in Math in Your Feet:

1. Stay in your square. If you have a question, raise your hand or sit down until an adult comes to you. Moving outside your square interrupts others' work.

2. Start in center unless you have a different idea about where to start your dancing (e.g., feet split in the front two corners, feet together in the back right corner, etc.).

3. No 360-degree turns.

Spend a minute with one student showing the class a 360-degree turn executed in one jump on one beat. Explain that it isn't that you don't think they're capable of such a maneuver, but that the classroom is too crowded to do it safely. Encourage them to try combinations of smaller turns instead.

Video Link 4.1

In this video I review the challenge ahead with a group of students, including a review of the movement variables. I also outline the basic rules and have one student illustrate a 360-degree turn.

http://hein.pub/mathmvid4.1

Potential Roadblocks

This is the most teacher-led portion of this process until you get to the transformation lesson. The goal is to give students the tools they need to understand the challenge and create their own patterns. Students may think you will be giving instructions the entire time, which might feel very demotivating. Periodically remind the class that you are doing this so the kids will have all the information and tools they'll need to make their own unique patterns.

Stages 2 and 3: Experiment ↰↱ and Create

Stages 2 and 3 show the dynamic relationship of the creation-revision cycle (detailed in Chapter 7). Children will experiment with the movement variables to create and revise their pattern A. When ready, they will then create a second four-beat pattern called pattern B.

While creating pattern A, kids are doing many new things all at the same time. They are getting used to moving in and navigating around their squares, how to coordinate their movement, how to combine the movement variables, and how to dance a pattern the same as their partner. They are also working as a collaborative team in a new context, and they are just beginning the process of understanding the idea of the dance pattern unit. When each team in the class has a pattern A and the partners feel comfortable dancing that pattern together, it's time to move on to building a pattern B. This is a really exciting time, probably my favorite moment in Math in Your Feet. Students have gained enough experience and expertise to fully embrace the challenge to make pattern B *as different as possible from pattern* A, and the room is often crackling with new ideas.

GETTING STARTED WITH PATTERN A

(20–30 minutes)

Goal: Experiment with movement variables and begin the process of creating pattern A. Become more aware of and experienced with the language of the movement variables and with using this language to identify the properties that make up your own and others' dance patterns.

Math focus: Patterning and thinking about pattern properties; unitizing; practicing fluid and flexible problem solving; using spatial thinking, orientation, and navigation; using geometric ideas in context, specifically the language, direction, and magnitude of turns; building an understanding of sameness and equivalence (by analyzing patterns by focusing on one pattern attribute at a time).

Key Points

Students work together to create their patterns and the teacher helps clarify the patterns, supports the collaborative work, and looks for places where students need support or new challenges.

> *We're moving to the next step up the ladder! Today we will focus on the joined steps of experiment and create. You'll work with your partner to make up your pattern and then practice it together. To do this, you'll experiment with the movement variables to create your pattern, but it may take a little time to get it just the way you want it. Your first pattern will be four beats and you'll call it pattern A. Your feet will hit the floor on each beat. Let's snap that out . . . one, two, three, four. You can make any kind of pattern as long as you're just using your feet. Remember, you also need to stay at "home," in your own square, and stay focused on the work you're doing with your partner.*

After providing the initial instructions, you have multiple roles, depending on the needs of each team or the class as a whole. In Chapter 6 I discuss in depth the factors at play while facilitating the math-and-dance classroom.

About five minutes into the initial math-and-dance making, you may be seeing some things that inspire you to pause the action of the whole group for reminders based on what you're observing. Sometimes a group will show me something that reminds me that the whole group could use the same tip. This could include things like the following:

> *Remember, if you need a break or want me to come talk to you, please stay in your square. You can sit down in your square or raise your hand.*

> *Your pattern A should have four beats, not counting your starting position.*

> *Your starting point is your "beat 0."*

> *Make sure you and your teammate are dancing the same on all four beats.*

Within the first five or ten minutes, a few teams will have finished the first draft of their pattern A. This is a good time to have the whole group stop and watch some of the new dance patterns. Bring up one pair at a time into your demonstration squares (or let them stay in their more familiar work spaces, if they like). Choose just two or three pairs of students in this round, with the idea that the rest of the students will use the ideas discussed in this observation time and apply the growing vision of sameness to their own patterns.

This is the time to remind students about the process (especially that demonstration teams are still in the process of learning to dance the same way), emphasize and be explicit about respectful audience behavior, and, if the teams can't yet dance together cleanly at a quick tempo (which is likely, since it takes lots of time and practice for most), slow their work down by having them dance each beat separately. This is also the time to start focusing on deeper understanding of the patterns by describing each beat using the language of the movement variables. For example:

> *Let's take a look at* [this team's] *pattern. Ah! It's interesting to me that you end your pattern facing in a new direction.* [To the audience] *Who can describe their beat 0, their starting position?*
>
> *Let's watch them dance it again and this time watch and see if we can name all the directions they use in their pattern. Where are they starting? That's right; they're in center.* [To the dancers] *Let's do this beat-by-beat. That means I want you to dance beat 1 and pause so we can talk about each beat one at a time.*
>
> *Who else is ready to share your pattern?* [Hands go up, but some teams have only one partner with his or her hand raised.] *Well, I see that a lot of you want to share your work, but for now both partners need to want to share. It's OK if you don't want to come up right now. Once you have practiced your pattern more, it's likely you'll feel more comfortable. But, just as a reminder, everyone will be sharing their work by the end of this project.*

After observing the work of two or three teams, send everyone back to work.

> *Before we look at more of the patterns you've created, please make sure you and your partner are dancing the same. If you do not have a pattern yet, please take some time to finish up.*

You may choose to do more observation later in your session. Most students will be very excited to share their work in progress, even if it's still rough. When all the teams seem to have something resembling a pattern A (meaning, something they can basically dance with their partner, whether it's totally clear or not), it's time to have an explicit conversation about sameness. This will help the teams now move toward an understanding of what it means to dance "congruently," meaning in unison with one another, all pattern properties the

Video Link 4.2

The class in this video has just spent about ten minutes working on building their pattern As, and I am curious to see their work in progress. Watch as both the demonstration team and the audience work together to build a concept of sameness between dancers.

http://hein.pub/mathmvid4.2

same; they'll need to think closely about pattern properties again when it's time to transform the original pattern into its reflected form.

INTRODUCING SAMENESS IN CONCERT WITH MAKING PATTERN A

(20–30 minutes)

Goal: Explicitly focus on how to dance "the same as your partner"; clarify patterns and identify movement variables.

Math focus: Identifying sameness, or equivalence, including discussion of relevant pattern properties (movement, foot position, and direction) and precise footwork and congruence between teammates; using spatial and geometric reasoning during evaluation of congruent dancing, including rights and lefts for foot placement and for direction of turns.

Key Points

When all teams have a pattern A, it's time to focus on being more aware of what they're doing and when. This effort is supported by a focus on *sameness.* As the first team gets ready to demonstrate, tell the class:

> *So, just as a reminder, we're watching the dancers to see what kinds of ideas they have for their pattern A but also to start figuring out what it really means to dance the same as our teammate.*

As in Video 4.2, I also sometimes simply ask the kids to see what they notice about the pattern.

At this point in the process the dancing will be brand-new to everyone. Your work during these observation periods is to help the demo teams clarify their footwork by making observations and asking questions such as this:

> *Hmm. It seems that Anna is splitting her feet to the right diagonal, and, Jordan, your feet look like they're split to the side. Which one did you decide on?* [You can also ask the audience to weigh in with a question like "There's something here that doesn't look the same to me. What do you think?"]

After you have watched one or two teams, if sameness has not yet come up in conversation with the class, check in with the whole group by asking:

> *So, what kinds of things do you think need to be the same about the pattern you are dancing with your partner?*

Video Link 4.3

The children in this video work to answer my question, "If I'm asking you to dance the same way as your partner, what exactly has to be the same?" They also evaluate a team of dancers and point out what is and isn't the same.

http://hein.pub/mathmvid4.3

Talking Through Sameness

A conversation on what we can "see" in the math-and-dance patterns, especially sameness, never goes the same way twice, though there are commonalities. Here is an example of a conversation I had with a class that was in the very early stages of working to understand what it means to dance the pattern the same as one's partner. You can also observe how I guide students to think about sameness and similarity in their own and others' work in many of the video clips accompanying this book.

> **Me:** *Let's say what we noticed about that pattern* [that the demo team just danced].
>
> **Jamiyah:** *They're both doing the same thing and they're not off beat.*
>
> **Me:** *OK, so by "same," do you mean same tempo? Did you mean same in any other way?* [To class] *Jamiyah was seeing same in the tempo, the same speed. What else did you notice about their pattern? Let's watch it again.*
>
> **Denell:** *That they've got a really good rhythm, like how they do it.*
>
> **Me:** *So we've talked about the tempo. What else did you notice?*
>
> **Tailor:** *That they were doing it together. They weren't, like one person wasn't doing different things. They were all together.*
>
> **Me:** *OK, so when you say "all together," what does it mean? People were saying they were dancing together. So what does it mean to be "all together"? What words will help us describe a pattern that is all together? What kinds of things can we identify?*
>
> **Kids:** [Start picking words kind of randomly from our word board] *Ooh! Symmetry.*
>
> **Me:** *Interesting. But what have we been talking about in terms of how the patterns have been made? What kinds of things are we using to build our patterns that we could also use to say if a pattern was being danced the same or not?*
>
> **Ayden:** *Ummm, transform?*
>
> **Me:** *No . . . we haven't actually talked about that yet.*
>
> **Amina:** *Reflect or . . .*
>
> **Me:** *You know, I've been spending most of my time when I'm up at the front of the classroom near these posters* [pointing to the "Movement Variables" and "Turns" charts]. *This is the information that I'd like you to think about. What kind of words on these posters might help you describe these patterns?* [Long pause.]
>
> **Maggie:** *Movements?*

Video Link 4.4

In this video, I continue to point back to the three different categories of movement variables in an effort to help the class develop its capacity for describing the moving patterns and build an awareness of how each beat can be described in multiple ways.

http://hein.pub/mathmvid4.4

Me: *Yeah!* [Talking to the demo team] *Did you guys do mostly jumps? Were the jumps the same on every beat?* [Bringing the demo team back up to the front] *Let's say "jump" for each beat while they dance.* [Team dances again.] *Now there was another movement in there. Look up at the list.*

Bryce: *Turn?*

Me: *Turn! Right! Let's say "jump, jump, jump, jump and turn." And how far did they turn? If they went from front to back?*

Kids: *One hundred eighty!*

Me: *Now, let's look at their foot positions. Let's do it slowly. We can also describe the sameness of their dance by looking at their foot positions. Right now they're together. Do the first beat and stop. Is that split, together, right, left, or cross?*

Kids: *Split.*

Me: *So let's see their second beat. Ready, go. What are their feet doing now?*

Kids: *Split.*

Me: *Where's their third beat?*

Kids: *Split.*

Me: *Good! You're staying in this category of foot position. . . . And where's the fourth beat? Split! Did they do four splits? My goodness. Let's watch this pattern one more time and let's talk about their direction. So their beat 0 is where? Center. So for the first beat, the direction is what?*

Dashiel: *Diagonal.*

Me: *Thank you! Is it a right diagonal or a left diagonal, do you think?*

Josue: *Right.*

Me: *Now let's look at the next direction. They went to the . . .*

Kids: *Side.*

Me: *The right side! And now the third direction? It looks like they went to a different kind of side with their feet to the right and left. Give them a round of applause! So what I'd like everyone to do right now is go back to your work with your partner and we need to make sure that everyone has the same pattern as their partner.*

The next observation session might start with: "Let's look at this pattern and see what we notice." If they notice something like a jump, immediately connect it to the movement category: "A jump! What category does jump belong to? . . . Let's look at the pattern again and see if they used any other movements."

Introducing and Connecting the Idea of Congruence

Depending on your students' experience with this geometric concept of congruence, you have a couple of options when it comes to connecting this idea to the dancing:

1. Explore the idea first with a relevant lesson from your geometry curriculum. Further discussion of this option can be found in Chapter 8 on page 157.

2. Another option is to discuss congruence during the math-and-dance lesson itself. After a few minutes of letting students review pattern A with their partners, sit the class down and ask students to compare their dance space with their partner's dance space. Students may notice specific inessential qualities like the color of the tape, or they might be more general: "They're both squares." Encourage them to get as specific and descriptive as possible about the properties in their observations and comparisons (e.g., "What do you see that tells you it's a square?"). If someone shouts out, "They're congruent!" right at the beginning, acknowledge the answer but continue pressing for descriptive answers (four equal sides, four corners/vertices, parallel sides, ninety-degree angles, etc.), so that the whole class can build the idea of congruence in relation to the dance spaces and the dancing.

3. Once you have linked the idea of unison and congruence you can say,

> *So, if you and your partner are dancing in congruent spaces, what do you think it means to dance congruently with your partner? What kinds of things need to be the same?*

Take some answers, but if they are slow in coming, ask questions that lead students to think about the specific properties:

> *If your partner's feet are split and yours are together, is that the same? No? Why not? That's right; they're not in the same positions. If you are jumping to the left and your partner is jumping to the right, is that the same? Why not? That's right; they're not going in the same direction. If you are jumping but your partner is sliding, is that the same? What's not the same about that? Right; they're different movements. So, remember, when you are dancing the same as your partner, your feet need to be in the same position, moving in the same direction, using the same movement, at the same time.*

The Importance of Language

The goal at this point is for students to move toward finding the most accurate words to describe what they and others are doing as well as understanding and naming the categories in use. At the beginning, they will understand what to do when you say "jump" or "diagonal," but they will have a harder time describing these attributes in others' work, most likely because they have not made full sense of the different categories of movement variables. The teacher's role is to model the language in every conversation (as discussed in Chapter 6), emphasize and reemphasize the categories, and, slowly but surely, help students become more precise with both their movements and their language. Modeling and conversation is a useful strategy when they are learning both the physical and the verbal language of the math-and-dance patterns at the same time.

Potential Roadblocks for Pattern A

At the very start of making pattern A, don't be disconcerted if students stand around a little in their squares while they figure out where and how to start. This is not a problem; it's actually part of the process. It's fine for kids to be stumped, but if it looks like they're really not getting anywhere after five or ten minutes, it may be a sign of other problems. Here are a few ideas for helping troubleshoot teams who don't seem to have any ideas or who seem unmotivated to experiment or collaborate:

1. Give them suggestions for the first two beats and keep it simple, like two jumps or two steps in center. Then ask them, "Where do you want to go now?" Having that particular task of deciding where to go next will help focus their work. At that point, leave them to finish it up. Sometimes kids don't really know what to do when they have their own decisions to make, and this strategy of giving them the first two beats has been very successful in helping teams get started.

2. Sometimes, despite the best intentions, partner pairs have trouble working together. One may have lots of ideas and not allow the voice of his or her partner to be heard, which might make that person unwilling to follow along. Or perhaps both partners are having trouble working through a disagreement. Assess the situation and determine the type and intensity of the disagreement, and then help them figure out how to try out each other's ideas until they have four beats they both like and can do. Make sure to first watch what they have come up with so far. This will give

you good information for helping them problem solve. Here are some typical scenarios:

- *If one kid is taking over,* often the other partner starts to shut down. You can make your observation of this dynamic clear to the team and then ask the second kid if she has any ideas that she wants to share. Support the first kid in paying close attention to those ideas then suggest they each pick their two favorite beats or moves and put them together to make their four-beat pattern. Most groups simply need support in kick-starting their problem solving; you don't need to stay with them during the whole process.

- *If they each have their own four-beat pattern* and are having a hard time bringing their ideas closer together, again have them each choose the two beats they like the best out of their own pattern and combine them. It's likely this will jump-start the collaboration, and the final pattern will be something different and much more collaborative. None of this is atypical, by the way. Part of making pattern A is the process of becoming a team and sharing ideas with each other. By pattern B this is usually less of an issue.

- *One partner may be dancing faster than the other,* which may mask unclear footwork that the other teammate doesn't understand. In that case, help them dance the pattern beat-by-beat to uncover misconceptions or unclear footwork or thinking.

Video Link 4.6

It can sometimes take a little time for a team to get started and get used to collaborating with each other. In this video, I check in with two girls who have decided on their beat 0 but have not yet started building their pattern A.

http://hein.pub/mathmvid4.6

Exceptions and Misconceptions

Although you will give students three basic "rules" for their work (stay in your squares, start in center, and no 360 degree turns) the only hard-and-fast rule is no 360 degree turns. Here are some exceptions you can encourage if a team needs an additional challenge, and some expected student misconceptions.

- *You always need to start in center.* This is generally true for pattern A because students are still getting oriented to the space, and we want to make sure they know the location of center. If they come up with a different idea for where to start, all the better, but the point is for them to be clear about where they're starting and that that location is called beat 0 and is not one of the four beats of their pattern.

- *You always have to return to center.* Students can end their pattern anywhere in their square.

- *You have to stay in your square.* Yes, they do have to stay in their squares—except that every once in a while a team will decide to switch squares during their pattern or move out of the square on one beat and then back in on the next. I never mention this as an option, but I also don't discourage it. This is always an unexpected and exciting moment and often inspires others to follow suit. As long as the followers have their own unique patterns, the leaders in this technique can feel proud to have inspired so many classmates with their (literally) out-of-the-box thinking.

- *If four beats are good, five (or six or seven) are better.* This work is pretty flexible and open to interpretation (like switching squares). The only thing that is nonnegotiable is the pattern unit. One of the reasons for this is that four beats is the unit for the traditional dance styles on which the movement variables are based. The mathematics of the dancing is also based on this unit. A four-beat pattern unit functions just like an inch, a degree, or a minute as a unit measure. One pattern unit can be added to another to create a longer pattern, and this process eventually culminates in a full piece of choreography. To emphasize the need for staying consistent with the four-beat pattern unit, I encourage kids to practice their pattern A (or later, their pattern B) once and then pause before they start again.

Video Link 4.7

Watch as I check in very briefly with a team who has figured out a pattern A pretty quickly. I challenge them to think about revising their pattern by taking out some of the jumps and replacing them with different movements.

http://hein.pub/mathmvid4.7

Adding a Challenge for Pattern A

If you find that a team has created a pattern quickly and is able to dance the pattern together, wonder aloud something like this:

I really like that! I notice that you made it really quickly and it seems like it's easy to you. I want to give you a little extra challenge. What would happen if you added a turn? Or two turns?

Or, you might notice they are using jumps on all four beats. In that case you might say:

I like that you both have a pattern that you can dance together. I notice that you're using all jumps in your pattern. Since other people are still working on their patterns, what would you think about trying out some of the other movement options on our chart?

The students will likely shrug and say, "OK!" and head off to experiment.

EXPERIMENT ↶↷ CREATE: MAKING PATTERN B

(two 30-minute sessions or one 45- to 60-minute session)

There should be at least a day between making pattern A and making pattern B. As with many creative activities, the first pattern needs time to sit for a while, to sink in and make sense. Because of this, students will need a little downtime before jumping into the challenge of making pattern B, which is all about making difference.

> *Goal:* Make a second four-beat pattern that is as different as possible from pattern A.

> *Math focus:* Patterning; unitizing; practicing fluid and flexible problem solving; using spatial thinking, orientation, and navigation; using geometric ideas in context, specifically the language of turns; building understanding of sameness, or equivalence (analyzing patterns by focusing on one pattern attribute at a time).

Video Link 4.8

Listen to students brainstorm with their partners about how they might make pattern B different from pattern A and then share out their ideas with the whole group.

http://hein.pub/mathmvid4.8

Key Points

This is the moment for thinking outside the (figurative) box. All you need to do is emphasize *difference* and support those who need it in thinking more closely about their pattern A to discover what exactly needs to be different in pattern B.

> *Today you're going to make a second four-beat pattern called pattern B. Pattern B will be similar to pattern A because it will have four beats, you will work with your same partner in your same squares, and you will be using the same movement variables.* But *your pattern B needs to be as different as possible from your pattern A. Talk to your partner about how you might do that. What kind of things might you do differently?*

Ask the teams to share out their thinking about how to make pattern B different from pattern A and then summarize the process for them:

> *How many of you have a lot of jumps in pattern A? Raise your hands so I can see. OK, so that means that your pattern B should probably have* no *jumps. You'll have to use your resources up here on the wall* [pointing to "Movement Variables" poster] *to figure out what other movements you can use.*
>
> *How many teams have two or more turns in your pattern A? That means that your pattern B should have no turns at all. Also, consider finding a different starting position other than center. The most important thing is that pattern B is as different as possible from pattern A.*

Video Link 4.9

A class works to figure out the biggest difference between a team's pattern A and pattern B.

http://hein.pub/mathmvid4.9

Video Link 4.10

In this video, I ask students to reflect on what they "heard, saw, or did" while making their pattern B. I spend some time with one team to chat about how they made their pattern B different from their pattern A. We also get to listen in to another team as they have a similar conversation.

http://hein.pub/mathmvid4.10

Students follow the same experiment-and-create cycle they used for pattern A to make pattern B. Just like you did during the making of pattern A, circulate through the class, and when teams show you their work, ask them to tell and show you what they did to make pattern B different from pattern A.

Pause the action every so often to bring up a few teams so others can observe their work in progress. There will be even more surprising, confusing, or unique aspects of pattern B to talk about and analyze together. For example, you might see kids starting in the back of their squares, facing a new direction, or switching boxes. These are all challenging new situations to describe and provide potent opportunity to further build students' ability to describe the pattern properties and analyze moving patterns.

Comparing Pattern A with Pattern B to Determine Difference

It is useful to bring up a few teams of students to dance their patterns to (1) see how or if kids are thinking about difference, (2) reemphasize the need to think closely about what is different between their two patterns, and (3) provide the rest of the class with some food for thought about how to design their own pattern B when they stand up again.

Potential Roadblocks for Pattern B

It's okay, especially if you have a group that is gaining ground very slowly, to have students make up only a pattern A, but I generally still introduce pattern B. Even in a class that needs more time to process verbal language or coordinate the movements with teammates, most students *will* be interested in and able to create a second pattern, and the process of thinking about difference will be a very valuable experience for them. Although I advised at the beginning of this section to keep everyone together if at all possible, if you do have a group where most teams are struggling and want to stay focused on building competency with pattern A, it's fine to give certain partner pairs more to work on while you're running the rest of the class through a slower pace.

Adding Challenge to Pattern B

Pattern B is a very engrossing challenge that can be met well by most students. Some of my favorite pattern Bs have been created by kids who took a while to warm up to the process. However, just like with pattern A, there will be teams that finish quickly. Ask these teams to show you both patterns and explain to you what they did to make their second pattern different than their first. If it doesn't look that much different, do not hesitate to point out what you're seeing (or not seeing) and continue to challenge them to work toward difference. If it seems like they're really and truly done with B, then another level of challenge would be to get them started mapping or communicating their pattern A or B using pictures and words (see Chapter 8 for more on maps).

Planning for Reflection

To maximize the learning at each stage of the process, you should have students reflect with their partner at the end of each session about what they heard, saw, or did during the day's activities. It only takes a few minutes to have them share out to the whole group. Ideally students should also engage in written reflections on their activity and in word studies and begin working to map their patterns. More explanation, ideas, and resources for extending and connecting the math-and-dance work can be found in Chapter 8. The next chapter continues the process with combining, transforming, and communicating patterns, all of which will challenge students in new and exciting ways.

Chapter Five

Math in Your Feet, Part 2
Combine, Transform, and Communicate

I n this chapter I focus on the final three stages of math-and-dance making in Math in Your Feet for students in grades 3 through 6. In these stages students use their experiences from making patterns A and B to attend to the new spatial and mathematical challenges presented by combining and transforming their math-and-dance patterns and communicating their work through performance.

Stage 4: Combine

Combining patterns A and B into a new, longer pattern C will be a great spatial reasoning challenge for your students. Even your more fluid dancers will be well challenged and engaged as they experiment with combining different sequences of A and B.

CREATING AND PRACTICING AN EIGHT-BEAT PATTERN

(two 30-minute sessions or one 45-minute session with time later for some extra practice)

Goal: Combine two four-beat patterns (patterns A and B) to make a new eight-beat pattern (pattern C).

Math focus: Patterning; unitizing; using spatial and geometric reasoning; practicing fluid and flexible problem solving; attending to precision.

Key Points

When combining their A and B patterns, students must start the second pattern from where the first one ends, no matter where their original starting place (beat 0) was. It is very powerful for students to discover the transition point between the two patterns themselves. Have them practice their A and B patterns separately, focusing on their ending positions. When everyone has done that, introduce the process for building pattern C.

> *Today we are moving to the next step in our process, which is to combine. This means that you will be combining your A and B patterns to make a new, larger pattern called pattern C. If I put two four-beat patterns together, how long will my new pattern be? Eight beats, that's right! Let's snap out those eight steady beats with no pauses. Great!*
>
> *How many different ways can we combine a pattern A and a pattern B? Yes, we have AB and BA. What if I told you that you don't need to use both A and B? Right! AA or BB. Today your challenge is for you and your partner to try out all four different combinations to decide which combination is the best fit.*

When all the teams have experimented with all four of the combinations, sit the kids down in their squares and discuss what they noticed about the process. Here you'll read what early fourth graders noticed about their process. They discovered, on their own, some of the big issues related to this activity, which I was then able to emphasize with specific instructions. This is far more effective than giving instructions first. They said:

- "I noticed how we combined two patterns into one big one." (unitizing in action)

- "It's harder when you do the same pattern twice, like A and A together, because I finish over *here* and I have to jump to over *here*." (spatial reasoning in action)

- "We need another step [meaning a ninth beat] to get to our starting position." (This is a common misconception that you can address once students have finished noticing.)

- "You have to take away one beat to make it pattern C." (I asked, "Did you take away one beat, or did you take away your starting position?" and the student replied, "The starting position." This points to the need to make clear that beat 4 of the first pattern serves as beat 0 of the second pattern when two four-beat patterns are combined.)

Video Link 5.1

In this video I introduce how we might go about finding different combinations of our A and B patterns and ask students to think a little about the nature of a new, longer pattern.

http://hein.pub/mathmvid5.1

Video Link 5.2

Watch a team of two girls independently work out each of their four combination options for their pattern C.

http://hein.pub/mathmvid5.2

Video Link 5.3

In this video, I listen to children's ideas and thoughts about issues with beat 0 and how this understanding might help them create strategies for making an eight-beat pattern instead of one with nine beats.

http://hein.pub/mathmvid5.3

Video Link 5.4

In this video a team of two girls show their new pattern C to the class and have put four claps between the first and second pattern. With the class observing, I walk them through thinking about how to tie the two together with no pauses in between.

http://hein.pub/mathmvid5.4

- "When we did [our pattern] forward and then we turned and tried to do it the other way, it was harder. We were facing this way the whole time and then when we tried to start from the other side and look this [other] way, it was harder."

The ensuing instructions to the class should focus on sequencing and on identifying the challenges they need to address. The biggest challenge is that the location in which you end the first four-beat pattern may be different than your beat 0 position for the second pattern. This may lead children to say, "We chose [this particular sequence] because the others were too hard [or impossible]." If you have time to explore this further, ask the rest of the class if anyone else encountered the same issues. This may uncover that fact that many kids still don't understand that beat 4 of the first pattern is *also* beat 0 for the second pattern. It's also nice at this point to emphasize that sometimes it takes some time and practice to make a new sequence, or combination, work. Tell them not to settle on the easiest one until they've given others their best shot.

Here are some other reminders students might need midcourse:

- *There's no pause between the two patterns.* They shouldn't do pattern A, stop, and then start pattern B. The goal is to have a longer and completely *new* pattern by the end of this activity. They're taking two shorter dance patterns and putting them together to make a longer one.

- *While experimenting with combining A and B, you have to stop after the first four beats and* think about *where the first beat of the next pattern is.* That initial ending place is the second pattern's new 0, the new starting place. What do they need to do to move from beat 4 to beat 5?

- *It is OK to change either beat 4 or beat 5 in some way to make a smooth eight beats.*

- *If you only have pattern A, it's no problem.* They just need to make sure they can do it twice in a row to make eight beats.

- *Make sure your team can dance this new eight-beat pattern congruently.*

If you feel like the class is really struggling, you can bring a demonstration team up to model the process. Choose a team that has both an A and a B pattern with some turns that start or end somewhere other than center.

Work the demonstration team through all four combination options: AB, BA, AA, and BB. Start with AB and have them pause between the A and the B so they have time to figure out how to get from the end of pattern A to the first beat of pattern B. Do it this way for all the other options. It's fine if things are a little messy at this point; it's the part of the dance making that requires the most practice to get things worked out. Part of your job at this point is to model the decision-making process by commenting aloud. For example, you might say to the team:

> *Oh, that combination looked good; I like that. How did it feel? Not so good? OK, let's try another option.*

Or you could say:

> [To the audience] *Doing pattern A twice looked a little repetitive.* [To the dancers] *Do you agree?*
>
> *So maybe this team will end up choosing a different combination, but they won't really know until they have a chance to practice all the combination options.*

Potential Roadblocks for the Combining Process

The biggest challenge for students is that bringing the two patterns together makes something that looks and *feels* brand-new to them, mathematically and spatially. This roadblock is only temporary, but it means that they will need encouragement to keep practicing.

Adding Challenge During the Combining Process

If a team finishes quickly, it's likely that it picked the "easiest" combination. Sometimes this is because the team's pattern B was a natural continuation of its pattern A or the students had looked at the ladder chart and had already figured out that the two patterns were going to go together somehow! Whatever the case, quick finishers should be challenged to really dig into making the other three combinations work. In most cases it takes a little practice to make the combinations feel natural and easy. If this goes well for a team and they are still done before the rest of the class, put them to work mapping their pattern C.

Stage 5: Transform

The process of transforming an eight-beat dance pattern is a physical thinking challenge for students and an opportunity to embody the idea of transformation. Students need opportunities to experience, analyze, and observe closely how reflection symmetry is made. Reflecting movement requires students to think carefully about what needs to stay the same between two dancers and what needs to change. This complements and expands their understanding of reflection symmetry and the overarching idea of transformation; it also extends and deepens the ideas of sameness and difference that were first introduced during the making of patterns A and B. See Figure 5.1.

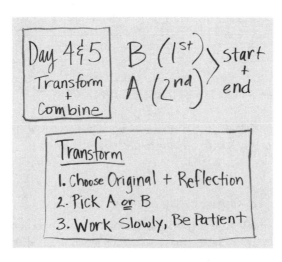

▶ **Figure 5.1** This image from my classroom shows one option for combining the final two stages. (See the Alternate Sequencing of Activities on page 103.)

CREATING REFLECTION SYMMETRY

(60 minutes or two 30-minute sessions)

Goal: Introduce mirror, or reflection, symmetry to transform students' four-beat dance patterns.

Math focus: Using spatial and geometric reasoning; creating geometric transformations; making reflections; practicing fluid and flexible problem solving; attending to precision.

Key Points

To fully understand the process of transformation in the math-and-dance patterns, we start with a familiar context (a mirror) and build understanding from there. Students will need plenty of practice time to understand and execute the danced transformation.

Be My Mirror (10 minutes)

Start with a quick activity to give everyone in the class a chance to think about what it feels like to be the reflection in a mirror. (See Figures 5.2 and 5.3.)

Divide the class into three sections and have everyone sit down. Have one section stand up at a time to be your reflection. Each group in turn should stand in a line, facing you, and copy your starting body position: arms to the sides, feet underneath you, legs straight. For the first group, use only arm movements for them to mirror (raise open hands, turn them slowly from front to back, raise one hand or arm while keeping the other low, etc.). You may see kids using the wrong hand. One way to quickly help them understand which hand they need to use is to try to match your hand up to theirs. Say, "Our thumbs should match; go ahead and switch hands. There you go!" For the second group, use only leg movements (slowly walking forward and back, bending knees, lifting one leg, sliding foot from side to side). For the third group, try arms and legs, plus a little movement from side to side, small upper-body turns, or forward-and-back movements.

▶ **Figure 5.2** Students reflect my movements. Here they have to attend to movements in both the front and the back of their bodies at the same time.

▶ **Figure 5.3** Students reflect my movements. Here they are focusing on matching a slight rotation and reflecting both arm and leg movements at the same time.

Same or Opposite? (10 minutes)

Next, have a whole-class conversation to introduce some key language related to analyzing what needs to happen when they reflect their dance patterns. Make sure to tape down a line between the squares in each pair in your classroom (including your presentation squares, if you have them) to stand as the "mirror line" before you begin this portion of the activity.

> *So, when you were my reflection, would it be fair to say that you were doing the opposite of me? What about the same thing? No? Yes? Who thinks it might be a little of both? To figure this out, who wants to come up and be my reflection so we can check this out? Stand in the box next to me. The line between us is like our mirror.*

Face your "reflection" and make sure you're both the same distance from the line. Talk your reflection through this so everyone can see and hear what you're doing.

When I look in a mirror, I am usually looking at the front of my body. Usually I look in the mirror in the morning when I'm brushing my teeth. So, if I start brushing my teeth by raising my hand, my reflection has to raise his or her hand as well. When my hand goes up, my reflection's hand goes . . . up. Is that the same or opposite? Yes, we're raising our hands in the same way. But, this is my right hand and that's my reflection's left hand. Is that the same or opposite? Opposite.

Now, here's something we don't think about all the time—the mirror can reflect all sides of me. For example, sometimes I turn my side to the mirror to see if my shirt is tucked in all the way or to make sure my shirt tag isn't sticking out. [Turn yourself to face the class and make sure your reflection follows.] *Can you see that I have one foot that is close to the line? I'm going to call that my inside foot. If I move my inside foot toward the line, my reflection has to do that as well. Is that the same or different? It's the same because we're both moving toward the line. But this is my left foot and that's my reflection's . . . right foot. Is that the same or opposite? Opposite.*

OK, how many of you have walked down the street and glanced at yourself in a plate glass window? If I'm walking down the street [start walking forward, as shown in Figure 5.4], *does my reflection stay behind and look at the coat she wants for her birthday? No! My reflection goes right along with me! So, if I move my right foot forward, my reflection has to move her left foot forward, which is the same and opposite at the same time!* [Make sure to walk you and your reflection backward with opposite feet back to the

squares.] *Now I'm done looking at myself in the mirror. If I turn ninety degrees to the right, my reflection has to . . . ? And now I'm going to walk away from the mirror and, hopefully, my reflection is walking away as well!* [See Figure 5.5.] *Give her a big round of applause!*

Video Link 5.5

In this video I use a demonstration team to illustrate how to apply the idea of reflection to the math-and-dance patterns.

http://hein.pub/mathmvid5.5

▶ **Figure 5.4** My reflection and I are both walking forward, but there are a few things my reflection needs to do differently.

Reflect Dance Patterns
(20–30 minutes)

Choose a team whose pattern A or B will demonstrate opposite rights and lefts (crossed feet, diagonal moves, and turns will do this). Bring that team to the front of the classroom or have the other students turn their bodies to face them in their dance spaces.

> *Everything the team does right now is for your benefit, so that you will know what to do to reflect your pattern. The first step is for you to be able to dance the pattern congruently. Dance your pattern beat-by-beat.*

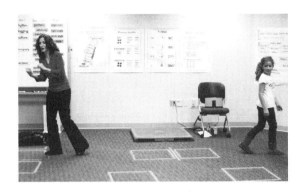

▶ **Figure 5.5** In this part of the demonstration my reflection and I are both walking away from the mirror line. However, our feet are not reflected because our backs were turned and our focus in this moment was the movement away from the line.

Ask your demonstration team to decide who will be the reflection and who will perform the original pattern. While they are deciding, have the rest of the teams decide which roles they will play when it's time for them to transform their own patterns. Have the original partner dance one beat at a time with a pause after each beat while the reflection partner figures out how or if to change the pattern. For example, if the original splits his feet on the right diagonal, the reflection will have to split her feet on the left diagonal and may or may not need a second to figure this out. Have the rest of the class help them figure it out and then have the team do the whole pattern up to speed with the mirror symmetry. Before getting all the teams working on this, remind them that if they are the original partner, they will need to move slowly for the reflection to be able to change the pattern. The person being the reflection has the harder job because he or she needs to switch back and forth between both versions of the pattern. See Figure 5.6.

Give students time to work out the reflection in either their pattern A or their pattern B. If it seems like they are getting it, ask the teams questions like these:

> *Which one of you is the reflection?*

> *What did the reflection need to do differently?*

> *Can you do your pattern both reflected and not reflected?*

▶ **Figure 5.6** This boy's partner was absent on the day we transformed our patterns with a reflection, so I took on the role of the original and he was the reflection.

The following conversation illustrates really well the kinds of things kids need to consider, both in language and in their bodies. It also helps them complete reflections in their journals. See Figures 5.7–5.9.

Video Link 5.6

In this video I check in briefly with a team that is working to reflect its pattern and has a question about what the reflection needs to do when there are side splits in a pattern.

http://hein.pub/mathmvid5.6

Me: *So tell me, what it is that has to change in the dancing? Please give me specific examples of what has to change in the pattern if you are the reflection.*

Lamar: *That your feet are doing the opposite.*

Rafael: *It has to be congruent. Well, it doesn't have to be the exact same, but it has to be very similar.*

Me: *So what is the thing that is different about the reflection when they do the dance?*

Elizabeth: *If the reflection does its right, the other person has to do its left.*

Me: *Whom is the reflection reacting to? Themselves or the original?*

Kids: *The original.*

Me: *So if the original puts his foot in the outside corner (away from the mirror line), the reflection's foot is . . .*

Molly: *Is on the inside.*

Me: *Really?*

Kids: *Yeah.*

Me: *Hmmm. Why don't you guys stand up so we can watch this. So let's say that you're the original. Put your foot in the outside (away from the line) upper right corner. So the reflection puts his foot where?*

Kids: *On the outside.*

Me: *On the outside . . .* [waiting for more information]?

Kids: *Left corner.*

Me: *So what else needs to be different? Is it just feet? Raise your hand and tell me what else it could be.*

Lexi: *Um, your like, body movement?*

Me: *Tell me more.*

Lexi: *Like, so, say this person twists this way* [gesturing to the right] *and the reflection turns to the left.*

Me: *Is there anything else that needs to be different?*

Ryan: *For, like, diagonals, then they have to be facing each other?* [Positioning himself in the square]

Me: *Oh! I see. So if you're the original, when you're doing a left diagonal (with feet split apart), the reflection would have to do the . . .*

Kids: *Right diagonal.*

Me: *And the body is involved because it's turned . . . how far? How far has it been turned from front?*

Kids: *Forty-five* [degrees].

▶ Figure 5.7

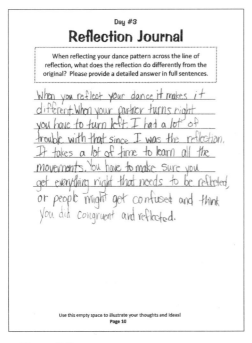

▶ Figure 5.8

▶ Figure 5.9

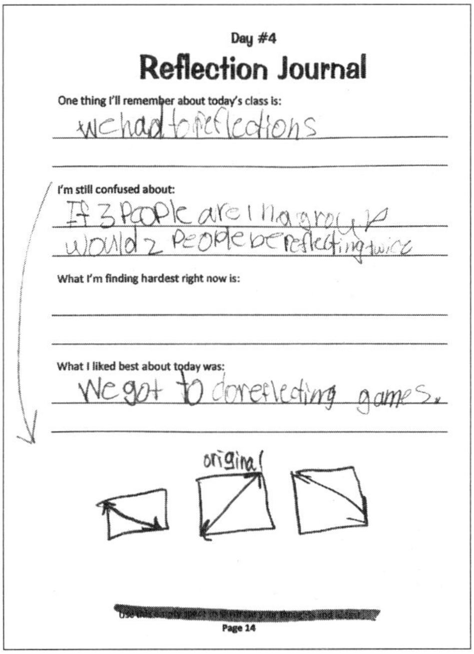

Playing Games: "Reflected or Not Reflected?" and "Who's the Reflection?" (20–30 minutes)

The games "Reflected or Not Reflected?" and "Who's the Reflection?" give students a chance to practice and present their reflected patterns and to assess how well they understand the reflection concept in this new context. They require students in the audience to give reasons why a pattern is or is not reflected and are a chance to further emphasize the differences between dancing with or without a reflection.

First give teams a chance to practice their patterns in both their reflected and nonreflected states. This should take five to ten minutes.

To get ready for the games, have the class look at a few examples of reflection in the dancing. If a team dances its reflection accurately (opposite right and left feet, opposite direction on turns), ask the class how they could tell the pattern was reflected. If one of your demonstration teams has some challenges dancing the reflection accurately, ask the class to help the dancers figure out what they need to do differently. Looking at the pattern beat-by-beat is a useful strategy at this point because it slows the pattern down enough to focus on each beat. After you've had a few teams demonstrate, have all the teams rehearse their chosen patterns again with and without a reflection. Then announce it's time for the games.

The first game is "Reflected or Not Reflected?" (Use your best announcer voice when introducing the games!) In this game, students will have to decide with their partner whether they will present their pattern without a reflection (the same) or with a reflection (opposite rights and lefts). When they come up to play the game, they are not to tell the audience what they are doing—the audience will have to decide which way they are dancing and justify their decisions.

After your first team dances, ask the class what they think and why. Students might say, "They used opposite feet," "I could see it in their starting position," or "When Maia turned left, Dina turned right." Here are some examples of conversations I've had during this game.

Example 1

Mr. C and fourth grader Grace dance. When they finish, there are audible gasps from the audience, like they've figured it out!

Me: *OK. . . . Let's watch* again! *Was it reflected or not reflected?*

John: *It was reflected because when they turned, their backs were facing each other.*

Video Link 5.7

This video shows an exchange during a round of "Reflected or Not Reflected?" and a discussion about what is opposite about what the partners are doing.

http://hein.pub/mathmvid5.7

Video Link 5.8

Another round of the game of "Reflected or Not Reflected?" helps clarify the role of the line of reflection in determining whether a reflection is present or not in the dancing.

http://hein.pub/mathmvid5.8

Me: *So if their backs are facing each other, that has to mean what?*

Kids: *They're facing in the opposite direction.*

Example 2

Me: *Why did you not think it was reflected?*

Blake: *Because when they did a right diagonal, the other person did a right diagonal.*

Me: *What other evidence did you have to support your claim that it was not reflected?*

Jordan: *When they turned, they turned the same way.*

Example 3

Me: *Oooh. Surprise ending! What did you see?*

Katie: *When they, like, turned, they landed in the same place.*

Me: *They landed in the same place, but what did you notice about the turn?*

Darius: *They turned different.*

Me: *They turned in different . . . what?*

Kids: *Ways.*

Me: *Ways?*

Kids: *They turned in* [toward the line].

Me: *Did one slide and the other jump? Or was it more like they turned in different directions?*

Kids: *Different directions.*

Me: *Did you see that pattern?! You almost couldn't tell it was reflected. It was sneaky! And you didn't really know until the end! Give them some applause for the sneakiness!*

After you have played this game with three or four teams and you think the students are able to tell between dancing that is and is not reflected, switch to a harder game! This one is called "Who's the Reflection?" Give all students another minute to practice their patterns first both with and without a reflection. They will have to present their patterns both ways: first without a reflection (danced twice, with a pause in between) and then reflected. The audience members will have to figure out *who changed the pattern* and explain their answer. Here are some examples of conversations I've had.

Example 1

Me: *OK. Who changed the pattern?*

Jackson: *Grady.*

Me: *And why do you think it was Grady?*

Jackson: *Because after he did a pattern,* [his partner] *Aiden followed . . .*

Me: *You saw him following along? Ohh. . . .*

LaShawn: *Grady changed his body while Aiden changed his body the other way so the bodies were the opposite.*

Me: *But how did you know it was Grady specifically?*

LaShawn: *Because, for the last time I was glad you said it was the last time they would do it congruently because I didn't get to look at their diagonals. So, their diagonals . . . Aiden's was a right diagonal,* [when they were dancing without a reflection] *I think, and Grady* [also] *did a right diagonal.*

Example 2

Me: *Who do you think the reflection was?*

Tessa: *Aniyah, because Demarco turned the right direction and when Aniyah saw that, she turned the left direction.*

Me: *How many people agree?* [Hands go up.] *Was there any other information?*

Brady: *In the beginning it was, when they did it congruently, it was right diagonal, left diagonal? And then Aniyah went left diagonal, right diagonal.*

Example 3

Me: *What do you think?*

Luis: *It was Nolan.*

Me: *Who wants to give me a reason for why?*

Isaac: *I think it was Nolan because on the second beat his feet went . . . when they did it congruently, I memorized their feet positions and which corner their feet went, and then I was watching that corner when they did the other one, then that person would be the reflection.*

Potential Roadblocks for the Transformation Stage

The biggest challenge at this stage is that children know their math-and-dance patterns so well that it is often difficult to retrain their bodies to execute opposite rights and lefts. As with the combination stage, encourage children to practice until it feels comfortable.

Adding Challenge for Transformations

This stage is pretty challenging! But if a team seems to be able to consistently execute its reflected pattern, you can (1) ask the original to take on the role of reflection or (2) have the team reflect its other pattern (perhaps also switching roles).

Alternate Sequencing of Activities

Although stage 4 (combine) and stage 5 (transform) can be done individually, I have found that children have an easier time with the challenges presented if they work some on each challenge during a forty-five- to sixty-minute session. Here's a sample progression:

1. When all students had an A and a B pattern, I might open a lesson with a warm-up that asked them to practice both patterns and make specific note of the ending positions for both.

2. I'd then spend the bulk of the session with the reflection lesson, leaving the games for the next session.

3. To open the next session, I would ask students to practice their A or B pattern (whichever one they decided to transform the day before) both with and without a reflection. Then I'd head straight into the games and if there were any time left, I'd ask them to see what would happen if they put their A and B patterns together.

4. The next time we convened, I'd focus fully on the combination lesson.

Stage 6: Communicate

Communication is woven into every stage of the math-and-dance-making process, such as when students

- reason verbally and physically with their partners as they plan and execute their math-and-dance patterns
- describe other teams' work using the terminology of the movement variables
- reflect on what they notice and wonder at the end of each session
- create written responses to journal prompts
- investigate and make sense of the math terminology used during this work in structured word study
- perform their works in progress for the class

- map their math-and-dance patterns

- engage in a map exchange to see if they communicated their ideas clearly in schematic form

All of these aspects are integral to the learning process and are covered in detail in Chapter 8. For now, I'll summarize some options for the final aspect of communicating one's ideas in Math in Your Feet: some kind of final presentation. You can mix and match these options as you feel comfortable:

- *Each team presents its final pattern to the class.* The audience members keep an eye out for whether the team is doing two different patterns or two of the same and explain why they think this. You can also ask the students if there was a moment in the pattern that surprised them or ask them to offer an example of something they really enjoyed about the pattern. This is a time of celebration as a class to admire and acknowledge the lovely effort and interesting ideas that brought you all to this point.

- *Students share their patterns with or teach their patterns to a younger class.*

- *Teams practice their patterns to music* (see the suggestions provided in the Appendix) and then perform them for each other; one half of the class watches the other half dance to the music and then they switch.

- Ask your music or PE teacher to help you work the math-and-dance patterns into a larger piece of choreography.

Whatever you decide to do, celebrate the amazing work of every participant!

In this and the previous chapter I detailed the specifics of the math-and-dance making and the lesson progression. In the next chapter I examine the *hows* of this kind of approach and discuss the various methods that can help you in your role as facilitator of a moving, math-and-dance-making classroom.

Chapter Six

Facilitating the Math-and-Dance Classroom

I n this chapter I focus on the *hows* of the learning and teaching in Math in Your Feet, specifically ways of interacting with students, whether individually or as a whole class, as they do their work. I also lay out strategies for facilitating a moving classroom and make suggestions for supporting students with particular needs. These strategies are directly connected to the work of assessing student growth and learning as detailed in Chapter 8.

The Big Picture

In the appendix of their book *Radical Equations*, Bob Moses and Charles Cobb (2002) point to experiential learning theory, which is grounded, the authors say, "in the countless cyclical experiences in which people try something [the event], then think about what they did [reflection], then make improvements [generalize], then practice their improvements [application]. It would seem that we learn most of what we know [how to do], from language to cooking, to building shelters to live in, by application of this process" (198). This description of "countless cyclical experiences" perfectly mirrors the math-and-dance-making process in Math in Your Feet. The event is a movement task, such as "make pattern A" or "make sure you and your partner are dancing exactly the same way." Students then reflect on their work, generalize and apply these insights as they make improvements, and practice their changes. This all happens naturally while kids are working to meet any given movement task; if something's not working, they naturally keep working on and thinking and talking about their pattern until they've got it the way they want it.

Because this approach is highly kinetic, many people think it is primarily about the dance. In reality not even dance educators, in schools lucky enough to have dance class for every student once a week, make their classes solely about the activity of dancing. Yes, building physical skill is important. We want students to get a feel for the movement variables, be able to use them to create new footwork, and feel like they are stronger dancers at the end of the process. But it is not the only goal. Other important goals for students' work in the math-and-dance classroom are

- collaborating with a partner to make something new, a process that focuses on clarifying ideas and the physical effort to make those ideas show up in the dancing, and working through the rough spots in the collaborative relationship;

- identifying the math ideas present in the dancing (their own and others), including discussions of sameness, similarity, difference, and transformation and symmetry, which are explicitly identified as part of what it means to "do math"; and

- reflecting on their own and others' work in a way that shows understanding of and appreciation for how the pattern is built.

Key Strategies

The three key strategies for facilitating this kind of learning, moving, thinking, reflective, and collaborative math-and-dance classroom to best effect are

1. Understanding the role of feedback, facilitation, and practice;

2. Making language your focus; and

3. Building and supporting a community of makers.

These strategies will help you, as facilitator of the math-and-dance making, orchestrate the learning in your moving classroom. This orchestration is, in part, about how to organize the moving bodies and help clarify students' dance ideas and their understanding of the math they are using. But the strategies are also about helping students become more aware of their own learning and thinking.

Providing Feedback, Facilitation, and Practice

Feedback and practice are inextricably intertwined in the math-and-dance learning process. Practice helps students develop fluency in their footwork and clarify the intent of their movement choices. It also moves students forward in their understanding of the math ideas and how to physically apply them to this new experience. Feedback, whether provided by the teacher, by peers observing the work, or by a teammate, is what initiates and motivates the practice.

Peer Feedback

A teacher who used Math in Your Feet with second graders reflected on the benefits of peer feedback and collaboration: "I believe that the partner system assisted the students in the learning process. Each student had a buddy with whom to discuss issues, questions, ideas, and achievements. They did not have to wait for me to assist or assess them individually. Such a system adds greatly to the amount of material that can be covered during the class period. It also adds time for partner practice and gives them a feeling of accomplishment."

Being in charge of their work and the decisions they make during the dance-making process also helps young learners cultivate metacognition (analyzing one's own and others' thinking). A strong first step toward metacognition is being able to say what it is you did and why, and how the results of that action affected other decisions later on in the making process. We move students toward metacognition when we allow them agency to think for themselves, make decisions, and negotiate their making process with their partner. These conversations provide learners with opportunities to step back from the process and apply a new level of attention to their work.

Teacher Feedback and Facilitation

Along with the natural opportunities for feedback from peers, there are some specific times when a teacher needs to provide feedback to focus student teams on a specific aspect of their dancing, usually related to the math embedded in what they're doing. However, you do not have to be a dancer or the "expert" in this process. Your role is to provide students with a sense of the journey ahead, introduce students to the movement variables, and help students understand how the variables go together to make a dance pattern. As Sylvia Martinez and Gary Stager say about using a making approach in the classroom, "take a deep breath and ask, 'Is there some way I can do less

Video Link 6.1

This video illustrates the balance between independent work by students and feedback from the teacher. These two girls have been creating their pattern B and are essentially done, so I give them an extra little challenge.

http://hein.pub/mathmvid6.1

and grant more authority, responsibility, or agency to the learner?'" (2013, 70). Children get all three of these things when they are provided with simple boundaries (the taped square), an inventory of ideas with which to work (movement variables), a task or challenge, and three to five minutes of independent activity followed by three to five minutes of reflection on their work. Within this structure you can start and stop the creative work at any time. You can pause the action for thirty seconds to clarify the activity, to refocus students on the relevant goals, or to see who's done with the activity and who might need a little more time. You can pause the action for five minutes to observe and talk with the whole group about work in progress or practice identifying the movement variables in action.

You can also observe the dance work of individual teams and share observations, even going so far as to say things like, "I think it looks really awkward for you to end your pattern with your feet crossed. You don't look all that stable. Would you both consider maybe ending with your feet together?" Or, in response to a frustrated team, you might say, "I know you love that move, but your partner seems to be having a little trouble doing it. Would you consider changing it to something both of you can do together?" Here are some other examples of what you might notice and when you facilitate the dance-making process to help move a team of dancers forward in their understanding:

Video Link 6.2

This video shows me checking in with a team to see what their pattern looks like. One boy is having trouble executing split diagonals. I slow their process down a little and provide some strategies to help him remember his rights and lefts.

http://hein.pub/mathmvid6.2

- *Partners are dancing at different tempos but don't notice this or have not yet figured out how to solve this problem.* Count the partners in at a slower tempo. If they still can't dance together, you might suggest the teammates count the beats out loud together while they dance.

- *A team is working on a combination of turns and one or both dancers are not clear about the directions of the turns.* Point out what you notice to the dancers and then ask, "What direction do you want to go in?" If they still have difficulty turning in the same direction, you could tap their right shoulders and say, "Make a fist with your right hand [or put your bracelet on your right wrist]. That will remind you which direction you need to turn."

- *One partner is jumping and another is sliding.* Share this observation with the team and ask them to make a decision together about which one it should be.

- *The team has a three-beat pattern, likely because the students don't understand that their starting position is actually beat 0.* Say, "I think you have only three beats. Let's look at this again. Where is your starting position?"

Example: Pausing the Activity to Provide Information and Feedback

A class of fourth graders is getting started on pattern A. As is normal, some teams are literally jumping right into the action and a few teams are standing around, unsure about where to start. My ultimate goal is that both partners on a team will have the same pattern and be able to dance it together at the same time and move toward a definition of *sameness* in the dancing.

My first pause comes about three minutes into the action. Like teachers often do, I clap a pattern to the class to get students' attention and they clap back. Right away I take advantage of the pause in movement and voices and say to the whole class, "So, when you and your partner think you have a pattern you like, make sure that you are both dancing it the same way. In a little bit we'll take a look at a few patterns and try to figure out more about what that looks like. OK, back to work!"

The kids immediately start working again. I stroll around the room and watch the individual groups dance. Some are still experimenting, but I stop and look more closely at the teams that appear to have a pattern that they can dance together. One team in particular has a couple of beats that look the same, but I'm not sure exactly what I'm looking at. My philosophy is that if I don't understand what the kids are doing, then they probably aren't clear either. It appears they are splitting their feet to the side, but one kid's feet seem like they're going toward the diagonal. I approach them and ask them to show me what they're doing. They dance the pattern and I say, "Cool! You know what? I can't tell whether you're splitting your feet to the sides or to the corners. Can you try that again, but dance it a little slower this time?" After they finish their four beats, I point out that one was splitting her feet to the sides and the other to the diagonal. "In a minute we're going to talk as a whole class about what it means to dance exactly the same as your partner. I think you guys are going to have to decide whether you want to split your feet to the sides or to the corners."

Note that in the first example I stopped the work of the whole class for a little update about our goals for sameness. My experience has shown that if I give all the directions at the beginning, I'll have to give them again at some point. By watching their work, I knew that some kids were getting close to having their first draft of a pattern. That's when they need to really start thinking about what it means to dance the same and this was a perfect time to bring up the topic. In the second example, I paused a specific team of dancers to check in with them about what they were doing. By pausing to have a conversation, I was quickly able to assess the situation and provide

Video Link 6.3

At first, the boys in this video seem to have a lot of ideas that don't go together. Once I clarify their starting position and direction, it turns out that they actually do have a pattern A. We say the movement words while they dance it and, because I can see they've got a good grasp on this process, and the rest of the class still needs some time, I leave them with encouragement to keep experimenting.

http://hein.pub/mathmvid6.3

Video Link 6.4

In this video another teacher checks in with a team about their ideas for pattern A. The boys are about halfway to having a pattern, and Kathy's feedback and questions get them closer to a full pattern. Notice how she goes beat-by-beat and checks for comprehension about the turns.

http://hein.pub/mathmvid6.4

some feedback to help focus them on each other's work and move them toward understanding sameness in the dance.

Example: Observing Work in Progress and the Beat-by-Beat Strategy

In the same class, I've checked in with or observed from afar all fifteen teams at least once and estimate that about half of the teams have a pattern they can repeat, but their movements are not yet completely clear or lined up with their partners' movements. I clap to get their attention, have them sit, and immediately begin something I call "countdown to silence": I say, "*Five,*" and then snap my fingers three times (which the kids join in on). Then I continue, "Four . . . three . . . two . . . ," and finish with a drawn-out and hushed "one. . . ." Now they're all seated in their squares, anticipating what will come next. I jump right into the focused silence.

I pick a pair to demonstrate (in this case, they decide to stay in their own squares instead of moving to demonstration squares). I remind the class to turn toward the dancers and pay attention. "This is what artists call *work in progress*, which means they're not done with the pattern and I want you to be respectful of mistakes. Mistakes are a part of this process. We are watching this team because they will help us to figure out what it means to dance *the same*." The team dances its pattern A.

Since this is the first time I'm asking for feedback from the class, I scaffold these first few demonstrations by modeling my thinking process out loud. I tell the team, "So, that looks really interesting, but it looks like there might be one beat that isn't the same. Let's slow it down a little so we can take a closer look. I'm going to ask you to dance each beat separately. That means I want you to dance beat 1 and stop, then beat 2, and so on. OK, ready? One!" I ask the class as a whole, "What was the movement on that beat? A jump. OK, beat 2." I do this for each beat and then ask the class, "Did they both do the same movements on each beat?" In this case, they have. I ask the team to dance the pattern beat-by-beat again, this time focusing on foot position. On beat 3 they are stepping forward to the front of their squares, but one student is using her left foot and the other student is using his right foot. I ask the dancers to dance beats 1–3 at a regular, steady tempo and stop there. I ask the class, "So, on beat 3 are they both stepping forward? Yes? Yes, so that movement is the same, but there's something *not* the same about this beat. Can you tell what it is?" The students notice the difference is in the rights and lefts. I say, "Fantastic!" Then I tell the students who are demonstrating, "So, your practice point when it's time to dance again is to make a decision about whether you are using your left foot or your right foot on beat 3. There's no right or wrong; there is just a decision to be made. Let's give them a round of applause. Thanks, guys!"

Then I say to the rest of the class, "And when you are working to finalize your pattern A with your partner, make sure to pay attention to your directions. If you go right, your partner needs to go right too. OK. Who else wants to show us your pattern?"

Quickly danced patterns can be messy and hard to follow and analyze. Slowing the pattern down with the beat-by-beat strategy is useful for both learners and observers. When I paused each beat in this example, the dancers had a chance to clarify their thinking and notice the difference in which foot they were using, and because it was executed slowly, the audience had time to focus on each beat and movement individually. Slowing the pattern puts everyone in a better position to provide specific and useful feedback. I made my point about rights and lefts by asking the class to *notice the difference* between the two partners' forward step, and that observation, in turn, was enough to provide a useful practice point (essentially a suggestion or reminder to help the dancers move forward) for that specific pair and a hint for the rest of the class. In three to five minutes, one team of dancers had provided a useful in-context example of *sameness* that benefitted everyone in the class.

Example: Group Practice

The whole class is currently in the middle of experimenting with different combinations of their A and B patterns to make a new eight-beat pattern. This can be challenging because it requires them to think through four different sequences, each of which requires a different transition between the first pattern and the second. I notice that our session will be over in about fifteen minutes and there is no way I can check in with all the teams individually in the time we have left. So, I get everyone's attention with four claps. I check to see if everyone has gone through all the options; they have. About half have chosen a pattern C. I give them two more minutes to practice and then say: "Right now I'm going to ask all of you to do something a little differently than you're used to. I want to see everyone's pattern C at the same time. I'm going to count you in as a group and you will dance your patterns all at the same time. When you're done, reset yourself to your starting positon and I'll count you in again." I run them through the group practice a bunch of times while simultaneously circulating through the room, looking at different teams, eventually deciding to run them beat-by-beat. After all eight beats have been executed, I say, "OK, we're running out of time for now. Let's do all eight beats of your pattern C at a slightly faster tempo. Make sure you spend time practicing it at home or at recess so we can do some fun math things with it tomorrow."

Video Link 6.5

Two boys have created a dynamic pattern C, but on one beat they seem to be turning in opposite directions. I look at their A and B patterns separately and then at pattern C and ask them to spend a little time figuring out how they can both turn in the same direction into the back right corners of their squares.

http://hein.pub/mathmvid6.5

Group practice is a great strategy for a lot of reasons. Having the kids dance their individual patterns on the same beat as everyone else gives all the kids a structured practice time, provides me a chance to get the big picture of their works in progress, and allows me to provide feedback to individual teams. For example, I often use this time to provide quick, in-the-moment feedback when something catches my eye, usually about keeping their lefts and rights the same in their footwork or turns. Group practice is also useful when a class is having a hard time staying on task. There are just some days when a group of kids can't stay in their squares and focus on their own work, or where they all seem to be in the middle of an argument about something. On these kinds of days, group practice can help get things back on track; it can keep everyone so busy that they don't have any time to talk to anyone but their partner. As soon as one round is finished, I say, "Reset!" and then immediately start counting again. When I think we've done enough rounds (generally five to ten iterations), I have them sit in their squares. This leaves very little time or space for extraneous conversations. There's also something about making rhythm together, even very simple rhythm on the downbeat, that helps refocus a group.

Making Language Your Focus

Using language *in context* to label, describe, and analyze this work is one of the most powerful ways to help learners create meaning and understanding. Although dance is intrinsically nonverbal, in this particular learning context the goal for learners is not just to dance but also to externalize their experience in pursuit of a better understanding of what they're doing and why. The language is present in the peer-to-peer conversations that happen during the making process and in conversations between the teacher and individual teams or the class as a whole. The vocabulary is made visible on the wall or board at the front of the classroom and is present in the reflection prompts and word studies that accompany the dance work (more on these in Chapter 8).

"Both my students and I benefitted from having all of the Math in Your Feet charts available during the class periods," one elementary teacher wrote. "Many of the students at our school are not extremely fluent in English. It didn't matter whether they understood every word or not. They were too physically and musically involved to worry about every vocabulary word. However, those words can become part of their English language, due to the active learning taking place. We want all children to become more familiar with both the math and the dance concepts. What better way than

Video Link 6.6

In this video a team of dancers is up in our demonstration squares, showing the class its pattern. I emphasize the language by asking the class to describe the pattern using the words from the three different categories of movement variables. I also employ the beat-by-beat strategy so we can slow their ideas down a little and make sense of them.

http://hein.pub/mathmvid6.6

to actively use [the concepts] and feel them while saying and understanding them simultaneously."

Making language your focus means being explicit and specific about the words you use when you talk to students about their work. It's also about finding multiple opportunities to ask questions that are best answered using the precise language of the movement variables:

- Who can describe their starting position?

- How many turns are they doing?

- How far have the dancers turned? In what direction?

- Is their pattern C made up of two of the same patterns or two different patterns? How do you know?

- Is their dancing reflected or not reflected? How do you know?

- What do these dancers need to do to make sure their pattern is reflected (or rotated)?

- Are you sliding or jumping? Are you turning right or left?

By using spatial language and the specific movement variables, teachers can help make the complexity of the moving patterns visible to learners. Each individual beat is layered with detail; in each moment you can describe the action as a foot position, a movement, and a direction. When students have the appropriate language to describe these different aspects of the dance pattern, the class as a whole is positioned to engage in discussions of equivalence. How can one pattern be the same as another? Does it have to look identical to be the same? Two patterns with the same movements might look very different from each other if the directions or foot positions are different. But even if they look completely different, the two patterns share an *element* of sameness because they share the same movements. Talking and thinking about similarity are at the core of comparing, sorting, and classifying; they require math makers to sort out the noise (inessential properties) from the essential properties that define the mathematical object.

In addition to spatial language and the language of the movement variables, we also use other math terminology as we make and observe the math-and-dance patterns. To focus on the elements and language of the pattern unit, the teacher might ask: *Where are you starting? How many beats is that? Where do you end your pattern? Can you do it twice?* These kinds of questions make clear what the unit is: four beats in which your feet hit the ground in some way on each individual beat. Students also use the language of geometry, including directional and spatial vocabulary and words like *congruent, reflected,* and *turn* or *rotate* as they work or observe others.

Video Link 6.7

This clip shows a variety of facilitation strategies all at once. The class and I move from a group practice (detailed on page 153) into my countdown to silence. Then we observe a team's work, slowing down the dancing using the beat-by-beat strategy. Finally, I provide the team and the class with the practice point of counting together while they dance to stay on the same beat.

http://hein.pub/mathmvid6.7

Example: Observing and Describing Others' Work

After a group of students watch a demonstration team do its pattern once, I say to the class, "Now when you look up at the 'Movement Variables' chart, can you find one word that describes their movement? Just their movement."

Joey: [Raising his hand] *Umm . . . jump.*

Me: *Let's watch it again and see if there is any other movement word that might come up.* [The team dances again.] *Was there another movement you can find on the chart?*

Isaac: *Split?*

Me: *Well, split is a foot position word. So we're not really talking about where their feet are; we're talking about how they're getting from place to place. So, let's watch again. I will tell you there is one more movement word we can use to describe this pattern.*

[The team dances the pattern again.]

Maria: *Ohh!*

Me: *What did you see? They were jumping and doing something else at the same time.*

Maria: *Spinning and together?*

Me: *Yeah, what's the movement word on the chart that would be the same as spinning?*

Maria: *Turn?*

Me: *Right! When you're turning, mathematicians use the word* rotate. *OK, now let's see if we can talk about their foot positions. So* [pointing to the chart], *the question is, Will their feet be together, crossed, right, left, or split? Let's watch the pattern. . . . Can anyone find the words to describe that?*

Ally: *Split and together?*

Me: *OK, let's see where they show up. Ready, go!* [Saying it out loud to the class while the team dances] *Together, together, split, split. Let's say those words together. Ready, go!*

Everyone: [In unison while dancers dance] *Together, together, split, split.*

Me: *Great! Now, when we're talking about sameness, are they landing on the same beat?*

Students: *Yeah.*

Me: *Yeah? Are their feet going in the same directions? Yes? Are their bodies turning both to the right, not away from each other, not right and left? . . . Let's watch that again.*

[We watch the dance pattern again and I have a question.]

Me: [To the dancers, Lily and Jacob] *Is that beat to the diagonal or is it to the side?*

Lily: [Simultaneously dancing the beat and answering] *It's to the diagonal.*

Me: *Let's watch one more time.* [Team dances.] *OK, great! Now it looks a lot like they are using the same feet in the same place at the same time. And tomorrow we'll talk about the math idea that goes with that.* [To dancers] *Can you do your pattern a little more quickly?* [They dance.] *Good! Give them a round of applause!*

Every demonstration is a chance to focus students' attention on something specific. In this example, in addition to using the movement variables to make their own patterns, I wanted the students to get used to observing and identifying the movement variables in others' patterns. On the first run-through I saw that the team's pattern used a lot of jumps but also a turn. A turn is a special movement; it can't be executed without some other kind of movement (usually a jump or a slide) and can be defined by both its measurement and direction. By focusing their attention on the movement category, I had a chance to connect the word *turn* and the more formal terminology *rotate* in the meaningful context of an actual rotation.

Building and Supporting a Community of Makers

The most important aspect of a moving, making classroom is the celebration of ideas. American society as a whole values the singular achiever, the person who does or is better than anyone else, *by herself*, even if she's part of a team. But what is "better" in the math-and-dance making? For me, this is an irrelevant question. Yes, some kids are more fluid with their movements from the start, but there have been plenty of kids who were not great dancers (yet) who came up with some superbrilliant ideas for their patterns—ideas that made me realize I had never had a thought exactly like what they were sharing. Other kids are successful at making their collaborations work despite a partner who is not that into the activity. A dance pattern can be thought-provoking, surprising, or complex in interesting ways. A pattern may not even be all that interesting but, in its finished form, may represent the forward movement of a team who took a long time to get started and experienced some real struggles in understanding the activity. In a moving, making classroom, we also need to cultivate a useful attitude toward the evaluation and celebration of ideas. Using the language of the movement variables and specific math terminology, we can talk precisely about what we think about the pattern and why, which can lead us all to deeper appreciation of *the work*. When we make

Video Link 6.9

In this video I want to make sure I've seen everyone's pattern C before our class time is up, so I get the group up to practice. I tell the class what my plan and expectations are for this activity and provide in-the-moment feedback on the dancing when needed.

http://hein.pub/mathmvid6.9

Video Link 6.10

In this video I check in with a team of two boys who are working on their pattern A. Their challenge in this moment is to be clear enough about their pattern that they can both dance it the same way. I incorporate the language of the movement variables as we work beat-by-beat to clarify foot placement.

http://hein.pub/mathmvid6.10

our math-and-dance patterns in community, we are focusing on *ideas*, not on trying to be "better than."

Sometimes, though, kids will get upset because another team in proximity to them, or even across the room, has come up with an identical step. This is never because someone has intentionally copied their work, although this is what kids will say: "They copied us!" This is simply an example of how ideas move around the room when everyone is focused on making something. Scientists who have studied this particular phenomenon call it "distributed cognition." Essentially this means that rather than happening in individual learners, ideas and thinking are spread across a group or influenced by the environment. In particular, when moving bodies work on a task (whether on a construction site, on a theatre production, in marching bands, or in a dance studio), there is another nonverbal level of communication beyond what we are saying out loud that most people are not aware of. Students are part of the larger focus and energy of the classroom, where everyone is working toward the same goal: to understand and make something new.

So, when the accusation of copying comes up, it is effective to ask the teams how they can change the patterns they have to make them different from each other. You can also remind students that when it comes time to combine the A and B patterns to make a new, longer pattern C, no one will be able to tell that their original patterns were the same. If things get tense in the class, it might also be useful to tell the story of the inimitable and amazing tap dancer Gregory Hines, who once said:

> One of the worst kept secrets in tap dance is that we steal each other's steps. And that's what we do; we just rip off each other's steps! Anytime you see someone do a really great step you take and try to shape it *and make it a little different*. (1989; emphasis mine)

There is a similar philosophy and aesthetic in the traditional percussive dance styles I do. There are norms for how the dancing might look and there's even an (often unspoken) agreement about what makes "good" dancing. But within all this there is room in the traditions to accept and, yes, even celebrate the individual ideas and styles of the different dancers within that dance community. This is what makes a moving classroom hum with energy and purpose. *What cool things will we see next? Oooh, that's a nice idea. I wonder how I can use that.* The fact is that a good idea is a good idea, and we are all working together to inspire and support the development of interesting math-and-dance patterns.

So far I've focused on what it looks and sounds like to be the facilitator supporting a community of math-and-dance makers. The facilitator's job includes things like these:

- making sure everyone understands the challenge ahead and has the same language with which to talk about the work
- appreciating individual gains, no matter the starting point
- celebrating forward movement in students' work
- valuing effort, interesting ideas, positive attitudes, and participation
- not making too big a deal about kids not getting it right away but, instead, helping move students toward understanding

Considerations for Students with Particular Needs

Although Math in Your Feet is structured to be inclusive of all kinds of students, building and supporting a community of makers and learners also means making sure learners with specific needs feel welcome in the math-and-dance-making classroom. Math in Your Feet is, by nature, easy to differentiate from class to class or student to student because although the framework is set, you have flexibility in terms of setting learning goals (both physical and mathematical), expectations for finished work, and the duration of each activity period based on the needs of your classroom. However, you may have some students who need just a little more support or consideration to feel welcomed and successful in the math-and-dance making.

Students on the Autism Spectrum

While students' needs vary, some students with autism will have success in fully participating when provided the agenda for the activity so they are aware of exactly what will happen during each individual session. This might include discussing ahead of time the steps everyone will take to complete the work (using the ladder graphic shown earlier). The activity preview should also include information about how there will be both movement activities and time for discussion. It might also be beneficial to

- provide the student with a visual schedule of your lesson and talk it through step-by-step prior to the activity;

Video Link 6.11

In this video I've sent the teams off to review their A patterns and asked them to decide whether they are going to say movement, direction, or foot position words while they dance each beat. I come over to a team to check in and discover that before these boys can do that, they need some support in clarifying their footwork as a team.

http://hein.pub/mathmvid6.11

- discuss with the child ahead of time what the options might be for taking a break from the action, if needed, to avoid becoming overwhelmed or overloaded; and

- provide close support from another adult, if needed, or ensure the presence of a good friend as a partner.

Students with Sensory Defensiveness

Similar to children on the autism spectrum, kids who are very sensitive to noise and movement may be quickly overwhelmed and made anxious by the activity and noise level. In this case, planning ahead with the child about how he or she can self-regulate or make plans for taking sensory breaks will be very supportive. Noise-canceling headphones or earplugs might be useful as well.

Students with Auditory-Processing Challenges and Language-Related Needs

Math in Your Feet is a vocabulary- and conversation-rich experience. This includes many verbal interactions between teachers and students that may puzzle, confuse, or frustrate children with auditory-processing or expressive-language issues, as well as English learners. Here are some ideas for supporting students with these kinds of challenges:

- Although the activity is language rich, children with language-related needs will be supported by the sequential, structured, and predictable nature of the math-and-dance-making progression (supported by classroom posters and consistent use of vocabulary) and the nonverbal nature of the math-and-dance making itself.

- Make sure to stop the activity and conversation in the room while you give the whole group new information. It will also be helpful to parse your instructions out a little at a time. Assign a task by providing just enough information to get kids started and then add new information into the mix in small chunks.

- You can also make sure kids with receptive language issues are sitting in close proximity to you so they can hear you clearly.

- Provide small whiteboards and dry-erase markers, if needed, to help teammates communicate their ideas visually.

Video Link 6.12

A team of two girls has come up to show its pattern B work in progress. I spend some time with the class working to clarify the movements the girls are using. I then ask the team to dance its pattern A so we can compare it with pattern B. Because this is the first time the class is comparing the two patterns, I decide to focus on the movement category when analyzing how pattern B is different.

http://hein.pub/mathmvid6.12

Students with Physical and Mobility Challenges

A really wonderful aspect of learning math at moving scale is the fact that an outside perspective is just as important as the action and work themselves. For example, a team of dancers may not notice that they are turning in different directions. If a child is unable to physically participate in the dancing for any reason, there are some ways you can engage her in the highly coveted and influential role of advisor or choreographer:

- *Feedback and brainstorming*: Once the math-and-dance-making process has started in full, engage the student in watching and providing feedback to one or more teams. For example, if the challenge is for both dancers to execute pattern A the same way at the same time, the nondancing student should point out the places where the dancing is not the same and offer suggestions. Or, when it's time to create pattern B, where the focus is on making it as different as possible from A, the student might engage with a team in brainstorming or keeping track of what might need to be different for B.

- *Choreography and mapmaking*: Another role for a child physically unable to participate in the action is that of mapmaker. He can spend time composing his own dance patterns in map form, getting ideas from the dance work he sees happening in the room. Follow the links for Videos 6.14 and 6.15 to hear and watch one such student, Maddie, explain her maps and how she challenged students in her class by choreographing and mapping patterns for her classmates to decode.

Sensory Seekers and Children with Attention Issues

The math-and-dance making can be a vigorous process and is perfect for sensory seekers—kids whose bodies crave physical input to feel at ease. The highly rhythmic nature of the dancing (in addition to pressure provided when their feet hit the floor) provides quite a lot of sensory and vestibular input and actually calms sensory seekers down so they are able to focus on the conversations in between spurts of dancing. A similar process occurs for kids with attention issues. The movement focuses the body and the child is able to stay present and contribute to conversations in the breaks between the math-and-dance making.

Video Link 6.13

Sometimes kids get the language of the movement variables right away and are able to use those words to speak precisely about their own and others work, but for others, it takes time and continued reinforcement. In this video, during the very last minute of our fourth lesson, a class whose observations had not been very specific become incredibly detailed about what the kids noticed about their work that day. We celebrate with "four vertices of applause."

http://hein.pub/mathmvid6.13

Video Link 6.14

Maddie works on her maps and explains to me what she's been doing while the rest of the class has been dancing.

http://hein.pub/mathmvid6.14

Video Link 6.15

Maddie challenges two of her classmates to read a map she created, and I challenge her to create a new map for another team to decode at the end of the class.

http://hein.pub/mathmvid6.15

Students with Cognitive Challenges

There is no one right way to create or perform the math-and-dance patterns. This work is highly adaptable for many different learners, whatever the challenges. Some kids may need a little more practice or need to dance at a slower pace. Or they may need an adult to draw a picture of where their feet should go to help them plan and coordinate their movements. As I discuss in Chapter 8, success is defined by a student's growth *compared with him- or herself.* Some of the supports described for students with autism (such as providing a clear schedule and opportunities to take breaks) can also be valuable for other students as well. You may also want to consider bringing in your special education colleagues as collaborators for planning or class time.

Many of the strategies for facilitation of the math-and-dance classroom discussed in this chapter are also the strategies you will use to assess children's work and learning. In Chapter 8 I discuss more specifically how to structure assessment of student work and how to extend and connect that learning to other contexts. But before we get to that, let's take a look at what Math in Your Feet looks like in the primary grades.

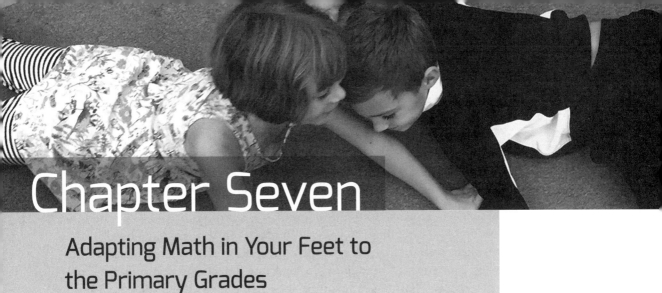

Chapter Seven

Adapting Math in Your Feet to the Primary Grades

C hildren in the primary grades are well able to engage in and enjoy the foot-based math-and-dance making but need a different kind of scaffolding and pacing than their intermediate counterparts. They come to the floor with different developmental needs both physically and intellectually and although the activity will look similar to the work described in Chapters 4 and 5, we need to adjust our expectations for both their learning process and the product of that learning. See Figure 7.1.

▶ **Figure 7.1** A kindergartner maps her pattern.

Key Issues for Facilitating Math in Your Feet with K–2 Students

Development of Physical Cognition and Movement Skills

In a very real sense, the movement *is* the learning for the K–2 students. We do also want them to use and understand the language used in the making context, make strides in representing their dance ideas on the page, and grow in their ability to work collaboratively with a partner, but it's the coordination of the entire body that creates the biggest benefit as they work at maximum capacity to get their bodies executing precise ideas in their feet. Your primary role is to help students develop the capacity to think mathematically with their bodies (as described in Chapter 2). Each session opens with a brief group warm-up that includes a short review of the footwork that you've done so far, continues to emphasize the pattern unit, and introduces new footwork ideas as applicable. For example, if you've already done jumps and steps in center and the children seem to be getting it, in your next session you might explore taking two steps in a variety of directions inside the squares.

Continued Modeling of Math, Dance, and Spatial Terminology in Context

Including mathematical and spatial language while children are engaged in their math-and-dance making is central to this work. Mastery of the language is a cumulative process that grows with each session. Observe yourself as you interact with the class while students work in their squares. Are you using both formal and informal math and spatial language while you comment on their work and talk to them about what they're doing? For example, you can describe feet split to the sides and then together in center in directional and mathematical terms as "sides, center." You can also speak more informally, but still spatially, using "out, in." *Center* can be interchangeable with *middle*. *Corners* can be interchangeable with *diagonal*. The classroom vignettes throughout this chapter will serve as useful models for how to weave this kind of language into your interactions with students about their math-and-dance making and learning.

A Slow Pace

Just like in the parable of the turtle and the hare, primary students will benefit from moving slowly and diligently toward the intended goal. This means introducing the movement variables a little at a time over many sessions. We start by standing with our feet together in center and stepping or jumping there; from there we add in foot positions and directions, slowly but surely, over multiple sessions. Repetition (even of what feels like the same lesson) and practice are better than pushing ahead, especially if it leaves time for observation of work in progress and discussions about that work. I've detailed suggested lesson progressions later in the chapter.

Clear, Consistent, and Patient Expectations About the Dance Pattern Unit

You can communicate the expectation of the pattern unit while talking with individual students and during whole-group discussions. You'll initially emphasize a two-beat sequence, but it's likely that some kids will keep going and make it four or six beats. "We're still thinking about *two* right now," you might say. "We're still practicing *two*. In a minute we'll see how we can put two twos together into a new pattern." This is also an unparalleled opportunity for students to develop a visceral sense of *two* and *four* as a unit.

A Pared-Down Emphasis on Sameness

In the K–2 context, sameness means *reproducing the same two or four beats every time you dance it* (which is actually a valuable challenge for this age group). It can also mean *dancing the same four-beat pattern as your partner*. However, if it seems like a student can't get both, the first priority should be remembering and reproducing the same pattern every time he or she dances.

Written and Visual Reflections After Each Session

Making dance patterns and mapping them are mutually beneficial activities and are key to helping students think themselves into the dancing. You can informally model the basic elements of mapping the footwork on the board while you're talking about where feet are placed (split or together when jumping or one foot at a time when stepping). I draw four squares on the board and use a circle in the center of the first square to indicate the starting location (in center with feet together). I usually use dots to indicate foot position and sometimes use arrows. Many students take these initial ideas and put them to good use, eventually realizing that they need a larger symbolic inventory to communicate their ideas in mapped form. This then leads to all sorts of wonderful invented mathematical notation. As I discuss more in Chapter 8, students should map out and write about the pattern they worked on that day at the end of each session. As you'll see throughout this chapter, these maps allow us an amazing window into children's thinking about their math-and-dance work.

Flexible Lesson Progression and Scaffolded Collaboration

Kindergarten and first-grade students will benefit from fifteen- to thirty-minute sessions. For second graders, forty minutes seems to be the optimal length. I've sequenced the K–2 activities to make them easy to start and stop at any point given the particular needs of your class as a whole. This spirit of flexible expectations can also extend to individuals within your classroom community. For example, instead of having students collaborate in teams of two, you might decide to scaffold the process by having kids work individually, then teach their pattern to a classmate before they begin to work collaboratively in teams of two. Or, you might start with teams of two and make a mid-course decision to have partners of certain teams work on separate patterns side by side. See Figure 7.2.

The main goal is to create and communicate a four-beat, foot-based pattern. If some kids are having challenges communicating with each other to the point of not having anything to show for it, then it's worth taking collaboration off the table so

▶ **Figure 7.2** A kindergarten student reflects on his first day of Math in Your Feet by illustrating the new structure and organization of taped dance spaces in his classroom as well as demonstrating his spatial reasoning skills. It's clear he is also fulfilling the expectation for writing to the best of his abilities.

they can be successful in the math-and-dance-making process. Or, if your class is obviously enjoying and benefitting from the work but runs out of steam after fifteen minutes, then it's completely OK to slow things down. Since this is a new context for a math investigation, you might not know exactly what kind of pacing your students will need until the second or third session.

In the rest of this chapter I lay out a lesson progression approximating what you might do with your kindergarten, first graders, or second graders and when. I also provide classroom snapshots of what it can look and sound like at different points along that progression.

Getting Started: Jumps and Steps in Center

(1–4 sessions, 15–30 minutes each)

The first few sessions are for getting students used to the new math and making context. The movement challenges require a precision of thought and physical execution that is still emerging in this age group. You'll start things off by exploring combinations of steps and jumps in the center of the square.

1. Ask students to find the middle of their square and stand with their feet together in that location. From there you will lead students in jumps and steps (like marching in place), both executed on a steady beat in center to make individual two-beat pattern units.

2. Demonstrate the jumps (or steps) with two claps in between the foot movements, for example: jump, jump, clap, clap. The clapping emphasizes the two-beat unit and provides a pause in foot action between one two-beat dance unit and the next. (When you move on to a four-beat pattern, you will put four claps between each iteration of the pattern.) The reason for the claps is that children will often practice a dance pattern unit by running them all together (e.g., 1, 2, 3, 4, 1, 2, 3, 4 . . .). Practicing the patterns with claps in between slows down their thinking process to focus more closely on the unit, especially its starting and ending locations.

3. If you're working with kindergarten, keep it to two beats for a few sessions.

Things to Keep in Mind

1. Remind students to keep an eye on your feet as they dance with you.

2. Rehearsing the movements with their hands (two hands together for a jump, one hand at a time for steps) while sitting down is a very useful strategy for this age group. Usually when I ask kids to sit down, it means that it's time to observe others' work and have a conversation. It is also sometimes a response to diminished focus with their independent work and provides a break from all the movement. Having moments of not moving, along with a quieter task for the whole group to do together, such as a conversation or a quieter way to practice their dance steps, helps them regulate their bodies and pulls their focus back to the activity.

3. If you are working with first or second graders, you can introduce the idea of combining two jumps and two steps in center to create a four-beat pattern. Do this as a group and then have them practice the four-beat sequence independently. When they seem to have it, it might be time to ask, "How else can we combine these jumps and steps in center?" (See Chapter 2, page 26, for a vignette of how this played out with a second-grade class.) Once you pose a question like this, give them time to work out an answer independently. After two to five minutes of experimentation, sit them down in their squares and ask if anyone wants to share what he or she did. Make sure to record each new sequence of jumps and steps on the board so everyone can keep track. After every new sequence, have the whole class practice the new pattern, either standing up or by using their hands on their knees while seated to rehearse the steps.

4. One way to encourage, but not require, collaboration during these independent explorations is to create pairs of squares and put kids who you think might work well together near each other. They will not necessarily start as teammates, but this proximity may very well result in a productive collaboration. If your class is doing well in teams of two, make sure partner pairs are consistently matched with each other. This continuity will be helpful as you move forward.

5. Remember that it will take multiple sessions before it looks like they're getting it, but it is more than likely that they will be pleased with their ideas and with what they are doing even if it looks a little messy to you. We want students to enjoy the process, and there will be many chances for you to move them closer to the goal while still allowing them agency over the process and the product. You can celebrate and encourage forward movement toward precision and mastery simply by making affirmative statements such as, "I noticed your feet stayed in the square while you were dancing!" or, "Your third beat was really surprising to me," or, "I can see that you and your partner are working really hard to get your movements to match."

6. Future sessions can repeat similar content. It may take a few sessions to figure out all the different combinations of two jumps and two steps. During this time your students will continue to build their understanding of the four-beat dance pattern unit, and they will get a lot of good practice with the two main movements they will use for the rest of the math-and-dance making.

7. Make sure to have students reflect on their activity at the end of each session. You will find vocabulary words and reflection prompts in Chapter 8. See Figure 7.3.

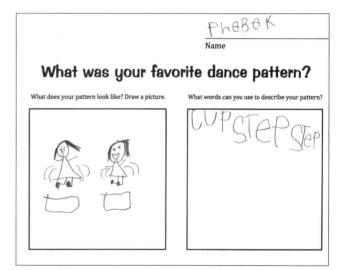

▶ **Figure 7.3** A kindergarten student reflects on her second day of Math in Your Feet.

Example: Developing an Understanding of the Dance Pattern Unit

At the heart of our efforts in Math in Your Feet is the dance pattern unit and all the mathematical things you can do with it (make it, change it, compare it, transform it, perform it). The challenge here is that K–2 kids are still developing a sense of wholes and parts. It's especially interesting to observe their work when they are challenged to (1) dance a pattern with the same number of beats every time and (2) take a familiar pattern and reunitize it (like taking two jumps and two steps in center and experimenting with different combinations of those movements). Here's an example from a mixed group of kindergarten, first, and second graders I worked with.

To the seated class, I say, "I have a question. We have two different patterns up on the board. Let's do them with our hands, making rhythm on our knees: 'jump, jump, step, step.'" After rehearsing the first pattern, I say: "Good. Now let's see if we can do the second pattern. . . . Let's do it with our hands: 'jump, step, jump, step.'"

The kids keep going: ". . . jump, step, jump, step. . . ."

"Oh wait!" I say. "How many times should I do that?"

To have an understanding of pattern unit, we need to understand where it starts and where it ends, and it's clear they don't have it yet, so I say: "I do 'jump, step' twice, so there are how many beats?"

Some kids reply, "Four!"

"Let's try that together using our hands!" I speak and move my hands slowly. "'Jump . . . step . . . jump . . . step.' Good! Now, I have a question for you. Can you think of another way to combine two jumps and two steps to make a different pattern?"

The kids seem to have no problem with this idea and immediately jump to their feet and start working enthusiastically. I stop the group after two to three minutes and say, "Before we're done today, if everybody has a pattern that's new to them, I want to get it down on the board. Who wants to show your work?"

First-grade girls Jada and Jasmine show us their work while dancing and talking: "jump, step, jump, step, jump, jump, jump, jump." I write down the pattern using Js and Ss and then draw a line between JSJS and JJJJ and ask: "So if each pattern is four beats, how many patterns is that?"

Jasmine replies with "Two!"

At this point I know that they don't fully have the idea of "dancing four beats and then stopping," but I want to recognize their work. I keep their eight-beat pattern on the board and then say, "Nice! Give them a round of applause! Who's next?!"

Two little kindergarten girls, Summer and Amy, dance and talk their pattern out for us: "jump, nod, step, jump, nod, step." At the board, I ask the class: "So what was the first thing they did?" I get feedback from the class and continue writing down their pattern. Then I say, "And now my question is, Is JNSJNS the whole pattern, or is it two of these [JNS]?"

Summer tells me, "'Jump, nod, step, jump, nod, step,'" and I ask if that is the whole thing. She nods.

"OK, so we're going to call that one pattern, and I'm wondering how many beats this pattern is?" Answers from the group include *two*!

I say, "Let's count them," and use my fingers to point while I continue, "JNSJNS. It's . . . what?" (See Figure 7.4.)

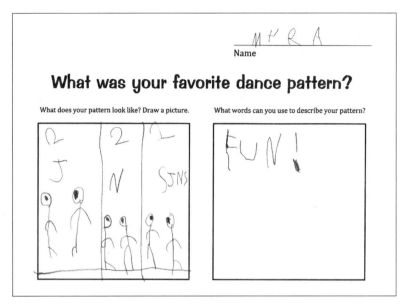

▶ **Figure 7.4** A kindergarten student's record of the pattern she made with her partner. She has divided the drawing space into three sections, one for each beat, and recorded the sequence of jump, nod, step. Even though she and her partner performed the pattern as JNSJNS it appears that she has an emerging understanding of the unit (in this case a three-beat unit).

Some students reply, "Two!" and others reply, "Six!" In a sense, both of these answers are correct. "Two" refers to the fact that some children are seeing JNS as the unit, danced twice. "Six" refers to the individual beats, which I emphasize next.

"Each time I say a movement, it's a beat. J, N, S, J, N, S. How many?" This time everyone counts six. "It equals six," I confirm. I point to the JS combos written on the board and say, "And these are four. . . . OK."

Adding in nonfoot movements other than the jumps and steps I'd introduced had become a bit of a theme with the kindergarten and first-grade children in this class (but not the second graders). Although I was being as explicit as possible about *what made a unit*, the K–1 kids in particular had been extrapolating that to mean *any kind of body move you can make on an individual beat.* I actually think this is kind of cool because they were thinking expansively about the movement. However, upon reflection, it did indicate a need for me to be clearer about the expectation for a foot-based dance pattern unit. The good news is that, just a few lessons in, it was clear they had the main point: they were using rhythm and movement to make their dance patterns; they could experiment and make new patterns; they needed to remember and

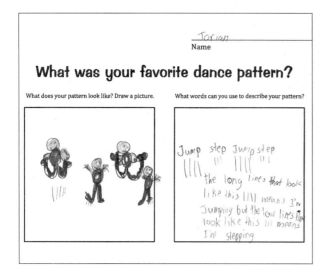

▶ **Figure 7.5** A second grader invents his own notation to emphasize the jumps and steps in the picture, and uses "long" and "low" lines symbolically along with words to record the sequence.

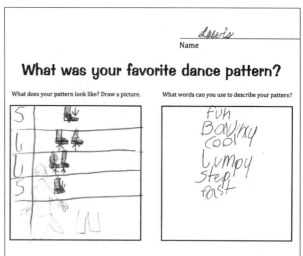

▶ **Figure 7.6** A second grader creates a structure with which to organize and sequence visual and symbolic information about his dance pattern.

repeat these patterns; the teacher would ask them to notice things and talk about their patterns; and there were special and fun new words they could use to describe their work. After a few more sessions of math-and-dance making, all their work was foot-focused. See Figures 7.5–7.6.

Moving Out of Center: Expanding the Inventory of Directions

(2–4 sessions, 15–30 minutes each)

1. After a warm-up with steps and jumps in center, tell the class: "We've been stepping and jumping in center, but now I'm wondering what other directions we could step in." Take one idea at a time and repeat it a number of times.

2. For example, if someone says, "Front!" you can say, while rehearsing the movements with your hands in the air: "OK, let's go 'forward, forward, center, center' with our steps. Let's do that together with our hands while we say those words." Repeat a couple of times and then say, "Now let's try it with our feet. Take a minute to practice that in your own squares."

3. In addition to stepping forward, replies might also include the corners, the sides, or the back. You can choose to do one new direction for combinations of two steps in subsequent sessions, or you can do all four options in one class. Exploring these new directions creates new spatial reasoning and learning.

4. Make sure that, in addition to the group work, you give students a chance to come up with a pattern they like based on the ideas used in the day's class. This may not be their final pattern, but it will give them a chance to practice creating and performing an idea that stays the same every time it's danced.

Things to Keep in Mind

- If you've decided not to formally pair students into teams, continue to encourage collaboration by maintaining parallel activity in the pairs of squares. This proximity may very well produce a beneficial collaboration. If your class is doing well in teams of two, make sure partner pairs are consistently matched with each other.

- If you have time, ask individual students or teams to share their work. This is a good time to provide individual feedback about footwork. Continue to celebrate and reinforce precise footwork and thinking. For example, you might say, "I was surprised when you stepped into the front two corners. I never would have thought of that!" or, "You just turned to the side of the square! What a cool move!" Don't be surprised if other children take these ideas and add them into their own work. Imitation is the sincerest form of flattery, *and* good ideas are worth trying out and then adapting into something new.

- Make sure to have students reflect on their activity at the end of each session. See Figures 7.7–7.9.

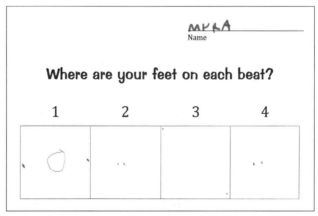

▶ **Figure 7.7** A kindergarten student maps her pattern. The open circle represents her starting position (both feet together in center) and the dots represent the position of her feet on each beat.

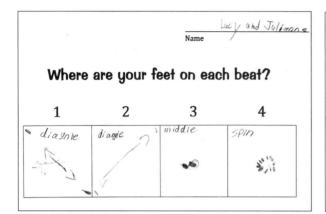

▶ **Figure 7.8** First graders work together to invent symbols and pair them with words to create the map of their pattern.

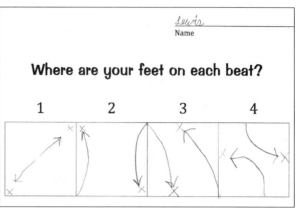

▶ **Figure 7.9** A second grader invents arrows and *X*s to indicate the direction of his movement and the location of his feet on each beat.

Adding in a Split: Expanding the Inventory of Foot Positions

(2–3 sessions, 15–30 minutes each)

1. After playing and experimenting with steps and jumps in various directions over the course of a few sessions, it's time to add in the new foot position of split. Demonstrate and have the whole group practice splitting their feet to the sides and then jumping them back together into center.

2. When they seem to have this move and can basically keep their feet inside the tape, tell them, "How else can you split your feet in the square? I wonder what we'll come up with!" Possible, and expected, directions include front and back (one foot on the center of the front edge of the square, the other on the center of the back edge) and diagonals (one foot in a front corner and the opposite foot in the diagonal back corner). It is possible someone will come up with a front-and-back split on the left edge of the square or something similar. That's cool too, and it provides an opportunity for conversation around the classroom definition of "feet split apart." Creating and debating definitions is a key element of thinking mathematically. If the opportunity arises, take it!

Things to Keep in Mind

- As before, give students a chance to come up with a pattern they like based on the ideas used in the day's class.

- Have individual students or teams share their work, and provide feedback. You can reinforce precise footwork and thinking with observations such as, "Wow. Your pattern has two splits, one front and back and the other diagonal. I wonder if you and your partner can make them look exactly the same?"

- Make sure to have students reflect on their activity at the end of each session. See Figure 7.10.

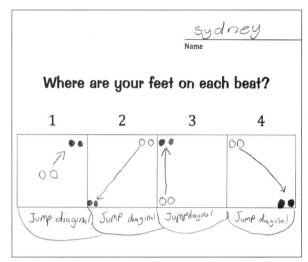

▶ **Figure 7.10** This second grader uses movement and direction words and a system of open and closed dots to communicate her pattern. On beat 3 she is using the word *diagonal* to describe a forward jump since it lands in a corner. A map like this provides an opportunity for a whole-class conversation about what kind of move or footwork is really diagonal and what is not.

Example: Adding in a Split

After warm-ups, I give the kids a new challenge: "I have something new for us to try! Let's put our feet out to the sides [feet split to sides, with a jump] and in [feet together in center]. But to make sure you don't step on your partner's feet, make sure you look at your square and don't go outside the blue lines. Ready, go! We go out and in."

I notice that the kids are all either in or out and clearly not sure about this new placement, so I put my hands in front of me and say, "Oh! Let's take our hands first and we're going to go out and in," while spreading my hands apart to the sides and then moving them together in front of me. The kids follow along as I say the words. "Good! Now say that with me!" We repeat the hand motions and say the words together. "OK, let's try that with our feet. Ready, go! Oh, nice! Let's try that again. Remember, when I say 'two,' the *in* is the end, and then we stop moving. Because here's the thing: *IfIjuststarttalkingreallyfastandIneverstopandIneverstopandIdon'thaveanypunctuationorspacesdoesitmakesense?*"

The kids reply emphatically: "No!"

"No! So we want our bodies to understand what we're doing. We want to understand 'two.' Right now we're doing 'two.' Ready? One, two! And try to keep it right inside the tape. Keep your eyes on your feet and your partner's feet. And make sure we don't go outside the blue lines. Ready, go!"

A girl spreads her legs much farther than the sides of her square, so I ask: "Are you inside or outside the tape? Let's try to be inside. Good. Let's do it again. I'm going to look at everybody's feet. Here we go: Out, in. Oh, that's good, that's good!"

Watching one girl repeating the sequence over and over, I add, "Let's do two and then stop!"

A pair of second graders raise their hands to tell me, "You could do it like this," and they demonstrate putting one foot in the front middle edge of the square and the other in the back middle edge of the square.

It's a great idea and I tell the class, "That's the next thing I wanted us to do—to think of all the different ways you can split your feet like that in your square." While I'm talking, the second graders are splitting their feet in different directions around their squares, and even rotating to face the sides and backs of their squares. (This is why I suggest that many second graders will be ready for aspects of the intermediate version of Math in Your Feet in the second half of the school year.)

I can tell kids are starting to get ideas, so I end our warm-ups, focus them on doing "out, in" to the sides a couple of times, and then say: "Now! I think someone has another idea for splitting their feet. I saw 'front [meaning a front-and-back split], together [in center].' Let's all try it. First let's do it with our hands." I demonstrate slowly while saying, "Split front, and center. Now, how are we going to do it? I put one foot to the front and one foot to the back, but we get there with a jump. So let's try that again." Everyone's got it, but one boy has put his feet diagonally. This is a great discovery! I say: "Wow, look at that, he just put his feet in the corners! Let's see if we can get our feet front and back and then we'll try corners. When we go front and back, it's almost like we're going to be on a tightrope. We're going to jump on the tightrope [*demonstrating*] and then we're going to put our feet back together in center." The kids do it with me and look like they've got it!

The whole class is excited and everyone starts talking to the person next to them and dancing at the same time. I want them to practice just a little more before I set them to work independently. I say: "Now, I have a question. Are there any other directions in our square where we could split our feet?" Kids raise their hands, but many are starting to move, so I say: "Show me with your feet. . . . I see corners; let's try corners." I turn around so they can follow and say: "One foot in a front corner, the other foot in a back corner."

Caiden, a kindergartner, remarks, "That's diagonal."

"And then you jump into it. Everyone try it with me. With our hands: corners, then center. Let's try that again. Let's try it with our feet." I talk and move at the same time: "Corners, and center. Now, look at your feet!" We practice together a few times and then I get the kids sitting in their squares and say, while drawing arrows on the board, "I would like for each group to practice sides and center and then front and back and center." I write a 1 and a 2 above the pictures. "This is one option, and here is the second option. What was the third option we just did?"

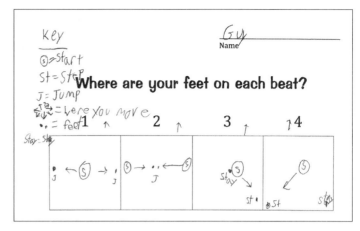

▶ **Figure 7.11** This second grader has developed a sophisticated symbolic system for mapping his pattern and has included a key for those who are interested in decoding the map for themselves.

Luis answers, "Corners!"

Caiden asserts, "Diagonal."

I respond, "And I say 'corners' right now because that's where each foot is going, but when you put both your feet in the corners at the same time, you do get a diagonal. So those are your options. We have three options for splitting our feet to try! Stay in your squares and if you have a question, either sit down or raise your hands so I can come talk to you."

Some students call out that they have ideas, but I know that for them to use the new ideas, they first need to practice the new physical vocabulary of foot placement and direction, so I say: "Oh! I think right now it's about practicing these three options for splitting our feet and *then* you'll have a chance to try out ideas of your own. You have a couple of minutes to practice."

The kids practice but get distracted by new ideas and directions. The first part of the session, as transcribed here, takes about sixteen minutes of class time. For the remainder of our sessions together, it continues to be a tug-of-war between the children's proclivities for settling on one idea and repeating and remembering it and for being inspired by new ideas in the moment. I continue to encourage practice of the ideas we have explored at the start of our lesson and, at the same time, celebrate new ideas.

Recognizing Progress and Wrapping Up

At the beginning of your work with K–2 students, things may seem a little chaotic in terms of the dancing and the unitizing. Children this age are notoriously (and wonderfully) known for taking an idea into unexpected territory. However, over the course of four or five sessions with consistent expectations about the pattern unit and the kind of language you use, you will probably start noticing things moving closer toward organization, including the following:

- more focused work in squares with partners

- many of the not-quite-participating, slow-starting, or on-the-periphery kids finally digging into the independent tasks

- good verbal and dance communication between partners

- a growing willingness to focus on and practice new skills

- a willingness to stay with the lesson flow (group work, observation time, independent work, written reflection)

- emerging ability to bring *both* partners' ideas into the pattern they work on during any given session

- a sense of agency with the material and more trust in the process (The directions and movements make sense to them and most of the students get that there is cool stuff they can do with these ideas and that these little pieces they've been learning can be used to make something new and interesting.)

When you start noticing these elements emerging, it's time to review with the class all the pieces you've been practicing and to have students begin making one final four-beat pattern either individually or as a team of two. This work will look very similar to their individual or partner work up to this point. It's just a matter now of highlighting the expectation for a final four-beat pattern that they can repeat the same way every time. The mapping cards (detailed in the following section) are a valuable tool for helping kids experiment with, settle on, and remember a final four-beat pattern. The cards are also very useful in facilitating collaboration.

Mapping Cards: Supporting Mapmaking and Collaborative Work

Collaborative work, especially when it requires a joint output, is not necessarily in the natural social repertoire of most K–2 kids. One first grader put it to me like this: "I'm six. I like to do my own thing." Fair enough! A big part of the issue is not only that they are still working to be precise with their footwork but that the dance goes by so quickly they can't quite catch each other's ideas. To support students in learning to communicate and collaborate with each other, make a point to have them represent or map their footwork visually after each session, even if it feels hard to them or is not always "correct." Partner 1 might be stronger at the mapping, and it's fine for Partner 2 to follow along on her own sheet as Partner 1 maps the pattern. After three or four mapping sessions, you might be able to further support both the mapping and the collaborative aspects by using the mapping cards I created, which you can download at https://mathonthemovebook.com or see pages xvii or xix for directions to all the video and resources. The mapping cards will work well with individual students and with teams of students (see Figures 7.12 and 7.13).

▶ **Figure 7.12** Two kindergarten students refer to their sequence of mapping cards as they recreate the dance pattern with their bodies.

- I give each team of students a starter kit of cards in a little plastic sandwich bag. (This kit will work fine for individuals also.) The yellow cards indicate the movement, either J (for jump) or St (for step). Blue cards are direction cues: arrows for split feet (two feet on the ground at one time) and dots for the positions of individual feet. You can also use the backs of the blue cards to draw in foot positions as needed. This tool is intentionally designed to not have all the information one might need to remember or reproduce the pattern. We want students to think closely about what symbolic information best represents their danced ideas.

▶ **Figure 7.13**

- Using the cards creates an interesting interaction between *what dancers want to do* and *how it's mapped out in front of them.* "Were you doing what was on the card? No? Do you want to change the card to match what you *were* doing?" The cards are semipermanent, flexible, and interactive because students modify, flip, turn, and sequence them to replicate in symbolic form the pattern they are making.

- Intermediate students don't necessarily need this kind of reinforcement to be fully oriented to the math-and-dance making, although they might have fun playing with the cards and creating challenging patterns for one another. For the primary kids, though, creating a visible *connection between* the dancing and the representation of the dancing seems to really support them in developing competence in both realms.

Example: Sides, Center, Window, Door: Map Reading with K–2 Students

Every once in a while, it's good to switch things up. If you feel like it might be interesting or useful for your students, you might consider seeing what comes up when you turn the tables on them and ask them to decode a map that looks similar to the ones they have been making.

I did this during my fifth session with a K–2 class after students had experimented with different combinations of steps and jumps executed in a variety of directions inside their squares. Their self-made maps were showing burgeoning competency to think precisely about the location of their feet while they danced. The Friday before this particular visit from me, five of the kids had been out sick; many were back but still under the weather, and four others were absent. Because of this I realized we needed something different than the high-energy math-and-dance making we had done so far. I decided to switch things up on them. I would challenge them to use their current knowledge of "what made our dance pattern" in the brand-new context of decoding visual and spatial information. Instead of translating from action to notation, I wanted to see what would happen if we moved in the opposite direction. Could they figure out how to dance a pattern by starting with a map?

Figure 7.14 shows the pattern I designed for this challenge. I am giving you a full version of the map with all the information. Take a minute to try it out. The pattern is not hard, but it will help you understand what happened next as I led them through transforming this map into a real, live dance pattern.

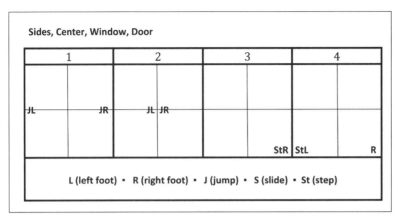

▶ **Figure 7.14**   Complete map for the new dance pattern

I didn't want them to be overwhelmed, so I broke the process down into a number of steps.

Step 1: Provide some of the information, not all of it.

Figure 7.15 shows the first map I gave the students.

After showing the class the map written on a flip chart, I said, "Look at the whole thing. We're going to spend some time looking, spend some time talking to our partner about what we notice, and then we'll get a chance to try it out." As kids started talking to each other, some of them gestured the foot positions with their hands as they talked to their partners.

One kindergarten girl came up to me and told me, "Malke, you missed a dot," referring to the single dot in beat 3.

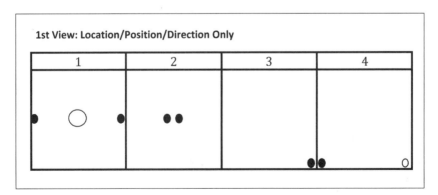

▶ **Figure 7.15**   First map, showing location only

My response? "Well, this is for you to figure out. Let's see what you come up with!"

Here's what they noticed:

- There was nothing in the front of the squares.

- In the third square, there wasn't a foot up in the left-hand front corner; that is, there was no diagonal.

- On the very last square there was only one dot that was colored in and one that was not colored in.

- In the center of the first square, it was uncolored, but in the center of the second one, the dots *were* colored.

After they shared their observations, I asked the class, "What do you think this whole thing is about? What do you think I want you to do with this?"

One student replied, "It's showing us how to write an example [of a math-and-dance map]."

Another suggested, "It's giving you an idea of stuff. Because if that's empty, then that's where you were." The student gestured the starting position with hands together. "But when you colored it in, that's where you are." She demonstrated the foot position on beat 1 with hands apart.

I addressed the class: "Can you tell me more? What does that mean I might want you to do with this?"

Alejandro, a kindergartner, answered, "Start there," and pointed toward the center of beat 1.

"And then what do you think you would do?"

Caiden said, "Go to the colored parts," and gestured with his right hand, showing two fingers split to make a V.

"OK, let's all stand up with our partners and see if you can figure out what to do."

Step 2: Let them come to an answer that makes sense to them.

As they worked on decoding the dance from the map and into their feet, my basic question for partners at this point was, "Does that feel like a good solution to you?" I asked this question because my biggest goal was to see how different teams were interpreting the map. Figure 7.16 represents some of the students' danced interpretations of the map I provided.

This solution showed up in a bunch of teams. So far, "jumping" had meant that the feet hit the floor either together (side by side) or split. The single dot on beat 3 made no sense if they were jumping, so the only logical solution at that point was to put both feet together in that position. It was

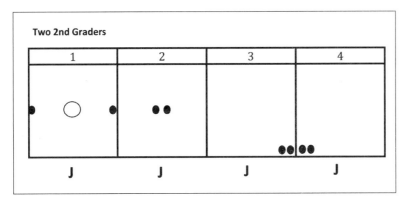

▶ **Figure 7.16** Several teams interpreted the map in this way.

also striking that although we had been doing both jumps and steps in our warm-ups and independent work, all the teams assumed that they were to jump on each beat. Two kindergarten girls (one of whom had told me earlier that beat 3 was "missing a dot") came up with a solution that was the closest to the intended pattern (see Figure 7.17).

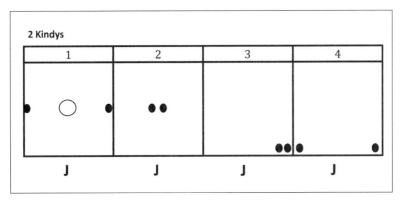

▶ **Figure 7.17** A team of kindergartners came close to the intended pattern.

Another fascinating result came from struggles with interpreting *forward* and *backward* from the map. The original map shows two individual dots in the back left and right corners. The team whose work is represented in Figure 7.18 read that information and put themselves physically in the front two corners. The reason this fascinated me is that most kids had, by that point, fully oriented their physical selves within the blue squares on the floor. They had also been successful in writing out their own maps (which I could interpret and dance correctly). Nevertheless, *many* of these primary-grade children moved themselves forward when the map indicated backward.

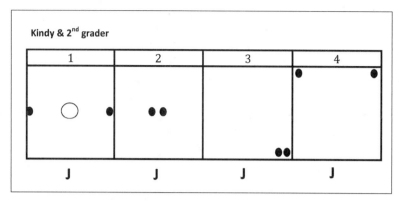

▶ **Figure 7.18** This team and many others moved forward rather than staying in the back of the square.

Step 3: Provide more details on the map.

I wish I could say that putting arrows facing up on the big math-and-dance map at the front of the classroom helped all the kids understand why they shouldn't move forward when the map read "back." Truthfully, what helped the most was adding one final piece of information into the mix. Up until this point, not one kid had even thought to ask what movements they should use. They had all just assumed they would jump. So I said, "On purpose I did not give you all the information you needed to do this dance pattern exactly the way I made it. So, do you want to see what I'm going to put on now?" I wrote a *J* under beats 1 and 2 and *St* under beats 3 and 4.

> **Me:** *Take a minute to look at it and then talk to your partner about what you notice.* [Students talk about noticing the jumps and steps.] *What does that mean is going to happen?*
>
> **Hunter:** *You jump and jump, then step and step.*
>
> **Me:** *OK. Does anyone else want to say that in a different way?* [Silence.] *What does it mean when it says "jump" under the first box?*
>
> **Daniel:** *Oh! So it means you're jumping to the sides* [splitting hands apart to show us]*!*
>
> **Me:** *Ooooh!*
>
> **Carter:** *And then we jump to the middle and then we step to the back corner and then you step to the other corner.*
>
> **Me:** *OK! Let's stand up and try this with your partner!*

After a couple of minutes, I told the class: "Let's see if we came up with the same solutions for this pattern." I asked a second-grade girl and a kindergarten boy to show their work. The boy watched his partner's feet very closely and got that he needed to be stepping in a back corner, but he went left instead of right. I ask them to go slowly. On beat 3, I asked, "Which foot goes first, the one toward the window or the one toward the door? Toward the window? OK, so we'll say 'sides, center, window, door' while they dance." Everyone said it with me while they all danced: "Sides, center, windoooowww, . . . door." And they got it!

Part 4: Use the understanding of some to support the understanding of everyone.

"OK, everyone," I said. "Put yourself in the center of your square, facing toward the board. Point toward the window! Point toward the door!" I corrected the direction of some kids while I moved to the front of the room. Then I had them mark out the dance steps with their hands while saying "side, center, window, door."

"We've got it! What are we going to call this pattern? 'Side, center, window, door'?"

The class enthusiastically responded, "Yeah!" and then we danced it and said it at the same time.

"OK, one last time. Let's hear everyone's feet dancing together. *Side, center, window, door!* Excellent! Give us a round of applause!"

To close out the lesson, I asked the students to map out the pattern themselves. I turned the classroom map over on the flip chart (out of sight) because I was just curious what would happen. Although not everyone was able to map out the foot positions on the outline I handed out, many of kids wrote out the words we used: "sides, center, window, door." Asking the class to decode a map similar to the ones they had been making turned out to be a just-right challenge for this group. To meet the challenge, they had to take their experiences with the math-and-dance making and their experiences with mapping patterns and apply that understanding in a new context, stretching their spatial reasoning abilities. If a child can recognize or use a math idea learned in one context and transfer and apply that understanding in an unfamiliar context (in this case map reading instead of mapmaking), that's good indication that he's getting a handle on the idea. I discuss more about this kind of assessment, extension, and connection in the next chapter.

Chapter Eight

Assess, Extend, and Connect

The body-based mode of learning I've described in this book is, by nature, primarily process-driven, and assessment of student work in this context is primarily qualitative, derived through observation and conversation with students. Considering both the verbal and the physical components of student activity is crucial to learning how students are thinking as they harness their bodies as tools for mathematical sense making. Although moving math lessons are ostensibly about students responding to a challenge and working toward an answer, the answer itself is just a small portion of what needs assessing. In this chapter I highlight ways in which to holistically approach the assessment of moving math activities. You can do this through observation and conversation during the action itself, along with opportunities for written reflection on the processes by which they met the physical and mathematical challenges presented to them and the words they used. Finally, by connecting the mathematical ideas as experienced and explored at moving scale to other mathematical settings, you provide yet another opportunity for children to deepen and expand their understanding.

Assessing Learning at Moving Scale

How do we know this kind of approach is working? What does student success look like? In this chapter I focus on the math-and-dance making, but much of the following discussion applies to the moving-scale math work as well. The main difference between the two contexts is the nature of the movement. At moving scale a child is harnessing her body's lived experience in the world for the purpose of mathematical sense making. In the math-and-dance context of Math in Your Feet, however, children are working within the system of percussive dance, a context that naturally constrains and focuses their movement choices and the challenge itself.

Defining Expectations for Improvement in the Math and the Dance

What kinds of expectations are reasonable for the math-and-dance-making process and product, given a diversity of learner skills and backgrounds? What are the most important skills and ideas I want my students to experience? The goal is for students to build rhythmic and choreographic competency using both the basic elements of percussive dance and math ideas to create their own patterns. This presents an interesting challenge for assessment. During this process children are learning to coordinate their bodies in new ways in addition to applying mathematical ideas in a new context. Assessment should address both aspects of this work with the understanding that success will look different for every child. This means a number of things:

1. We need to value and allow for a range of physical skills, knowing that children can and will grow their skills with practice and that, even within same-age classrooms, children's motor skills can vary drastically from each other.

2. Students experience and apply mathematical ideas (both content- and process-based) to their work, and their understanding of those ideas is best assessed through conversation, written reflections, and mapping.

3. Additional opportunities for assessment occur when we provide time and space for children to connect the math learned and used at moving scale to other mathematical modes and contexts, suggestions for which are found later in this chapter.

4. In addition to assessing the math and the dance, we also need to make explicit our expectations for students' participation in creating a supportive making environment and about the criteria for a final product.

Overall, my approach has always been about how far a child has moved down the learning road *compared with him- or herself*. Although many children have been successful in making math-and-dance patterns, not every pattern is objectively outstanding, nor does it need to be. I find the real evidence of student growth by keeping track of the path each team has taken to create its final pattern. Grading or judging a child on his or her ability compared with others' is harmful in this creative environment. This is a place where the focus should be firmly on the ideas expressed, not on the facility or ease of that expression. Our feedback as educators as well as feedback from others in the class should reflect this value—we all need to focus on helping the math-and-dance makers clarify their intended ideas and celebrate when they are finally able to do so.

You are assessing the gains a child has made in expressing herself precisely with her body, her words, and her mapped representations. The following sections outline how you can assess some of these things in the moment during the activity itself and others through written and mapped reflections as students spend time making sense of and communicating about their process and product.

Assessing the Math Within the Dance Context

Assessing the math learning in the dance context means you are assessing the mathematics as it is expressed in its dynamic, moving form. The math that is best assessed by watching the dancing in action includes spatial reasoning, transformation and reflection, unitizing, rotations, and the math practices of attending to precision and using tools appropriate to the situation. Here are some examples of the math that is visible while children make their patterns:

- *Precision*: The taped dance spaces will help you quite a bit in assessing precision. If students have created a pattern where the feet need to be split on the right diagonal, then you'll be able to see clearly if they've executed that or not. Noting their precision or lack of it during the process of making pattern A will clue you to ask them about their intentions with the pattern. It will also provide a useful benchmark for noting growth in this area by the end of the process. It's important to realize that imprecise footwork can also relate to low motivation, a missed breakfast or lack of sleep, underlying social issues, or any other number of nonmathematical factors. We want students to move toward precise thinking and expression in mathematics and this setting is the perfect opportunity for teachers to enthusiastically support and encourage them to reason precisely with their bodies. We encourage precise dancing by focusing on matters of equivalence. During observation of student work, for example, you might see teams who are not clear about their footwork. Asking the class as a whole to provide feedback for what aspects don't look the same, or asking the pair themselves what needs to be the same, is a useful way to focus their attention on this piece of mathematics.

● *Rotation:* Spatial reasoning takes practice, especially being consistent with rights and lefts and rotations. When members of a team are executing turns in different directions, it's often because the dancers haven't yet noticed these details. The challenge increases further as students combine patterns in different orders and again when they transform congruent into reflected dancing. Do students take feedback from the teacher or peers and make continued efforts toward accuracy in their rotations and directions of turns? Forward movement is the goal.

● *Unitizing:* Unitizing needs less attention in the intermediate grades than with primary students. However, when students are still in the exploratory stages of pattern A, you may notice teams making patterns with more or less than four beats. If more than a few teams are exhibiting confusion about the dance pattern unit, this tells you that the class as a whole needs a reminder. If it continues to be an issue, then you might need to back up a little and review the ideas of a beat 0 (starting place) and four consecutive beats.

● *Reflection:* The onus of reflecting a math-and-dance pattern is fully on the child who has to change the original pattern into its reflected version. This takes quite a lot of practice and requires the child to change some now well-practiced physical patterning. You can get a good sense of whether a child, or the team, has this concept by observing their dancing. Speed is of no consideration here, so if the danced reflection is not clearly executed, ask them to slow down their dancing. A slower tempo will clarify for you whether or not a child understands this idea or not. To assess the understanding of the teammate who did not take on the role of reflection, you can either ask her what the reflection had to do differently in the dancing or ask her to take on the role of reflection herself.

In summary, assessing math learning in the dynamic context of the math-and-dance making involves noting student gains in one or more of these combined math-and-dance skills:

● coordinating and orienting the body in and through space (spatial reasoning)

● coordinating rights and lefts with a partner in both footwork and turns (for intermediate students; spatial reasoning and rotations)

- moving closer to demonstrating clear movements, directions, and foot placement (attending to precision)

- improving ability to dance exactly the same as a partner (attending to precision and equivalence relations)

These expectations should be tailored to each individual team. There is no right or wrong dancing as long as students are working within the constraints of the activity. Sometimes, given social, emotional, physical, sensory, or cognitive challenges, creating and sharing a final four- or eight-beat math-and-dance pattern is the epitome of success.

Assessing the Math Verbally and in Writing

Although I keep my assessment of students' physical skills to myself and, in fact, rarely consider it useful beyond noting growth, I do make explicit my expectations for student contributions to the classroom community as both makers and mathematicians. I share these expectations at each new step of the math-and-dance-making process. Mathematically, students are expected to be able to identify the movement variables in their own patterns, which will lead, sometimes slowly, to an improved ability to describe and analyze the patterns of others. This is primarily practiced in the context of the math-and-dance making itself. Teachers can support the development of this skill by providing multiple opportunities for verbal and written reflections and for creating maps of their math-and-dance patterns and decoding others' maps. In his book *Experience and Education*, John Dewey wrote, "Every experience is a moving force. Its value can be judged only on the ground of what it moves toward and into. . . . Experiences may be so disconnected from one another that, while each is agreeable or even exciting in itself, they are not linked cumulatively to one another" (1938, 38). This is why we need to provide opportunities for students to reflect on their experience and, especially, find ways to build links between the moving math experiences through written reflection and word studies, making maps of their math-and-dance patterns, and other math learning contexts (discussed later in this chapter).

Written Reflections and Word Study

When children have the opportunity to reflect in writing on their making process and the words they use, they enter each subsequent stage of the process better equipped to handle the new challenges presented to them. The written reflections are best done at the end of each session, while the activity challenge is still fresh, and they should focus on the different aspects of the math-and-dance making. Students' responses can show you how they are integrating the language of the movement variables and other math terminology as well as their understanding of the mathematics in the moving-math context. Examples of written reflection prompts and student work are provided later in this chapter.

It is also hugely helpful for students to think closely about certain aspects of the terminology used during their math-and-dance making. The Frayer model for developing academic vocabulary is particularly helpful here (see www.readingeducator.com/strategies/frayer.htm for a good overview). Students explore each word in four different ways: they define it in their own terms, they record facts or characteristics gleaned from a math dictionary or other resource, they provide an example, and they provide a nonexample.

Students can respond with both words and pictures. You can work this into your current math journal format, create your own word study pages, or find premade templates online. Suggestions for word studies have been provided for both the primary and the intermediate versions of Math in Your Feet later in this chapter. See Figure 8.1.

Making and Reading Maps (grades 3–6)

In Chapter 7 I talked about and illustrated the role mapping plays in the primary grades. The mapping activity is how K–2 students think themselves into the dance work; because the physical challenges are great, their dancing improves with practice and the opportunity to think closely in a visual mode about the placement of their feet in the square. You can use these maps as a way to assess their growth from lesson to lesson because it is likely you will see gains in their spatial reasoning and clarity of expression. For intermediate

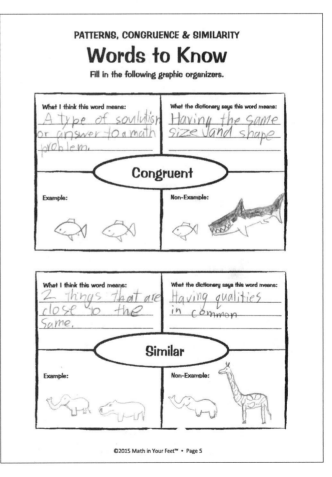

▶ **Figure 8.1** A sample word study.

students, however, the mapping is tied directly to two expectations for the communication aspect of the math-and-dance patterns, both of which will assist you in assessing the gains your students have made from the beginning of the process: for children to be able to communicate their math-and-dance ideas clearly to others as a final piece of creative work to the whole class, and for students to think about and express their math-and-dance patterns in multiple modes.

Making maps of math-and-dance patterns is a highly mathematical process that takes the dynamic physical representation of the pattern you've created, and the mathematics embedded within it (symmetry, spatial thinking, rotations, etc.), and transfers those ideas into a new schematic format. Lowell Miller, a fourth-grade teacher, said, "One of my big goals for Math in Your Feet is the communication piece. Certain students can rip through the dance, you can rip through any assignment and be done with it. Boom—I'm done. But when I tell them, . . . 'I want you to communicate the pattern in your feet, I want you to communicate your pattern verbally to someone else, I want you to be able to communicate your pattern by writing down the steps,' . . . kids have to slow down their work and really think about it and become more explicit and precise."

When children begin mapping their pattern, they have to think very closely about how to abstract the relevant properties of the pattern so that others can reproduce their ideas. Students will not only need to wrestle with the words and symbols needed to communicate the pattern as precisely as possible in a visual format but also need to attend closely to the sequencing of those ideas.

There are two separate but related approaches to making the math-and-dance maps. In either case the goal is for students to think closely about how to communicate their ideas clearly. The first is a structured format where the focus is primarily on identifying what words best describe each category of each beat of a four-beat pattern and includes an organized table in which students record the relevant information about their patterns. The second approach is more mathematical in nature, an open-ended process focused on children making sense of the terminology, spatial aspects, and sequencing of the math-and-dance patterns in their own terms. As a final test for both approaches, have teams exchange their recorded patterns to investigate whether others can indeed read them and dance them.

In the examples in Figures 8.2 and 8.3, the chart requires students to use the most accurate word for each category (feet, movement, and direction) on each beat of the pattern. Overall, the examples show a good level of mastery with the language of the movement variables, but they also exhibit a need for revision and clarification.

The next series of maps were created by Lowell Miller's fourth graders with the explicit expectation for accurate and clear sequencing of ideas. What I appreciate about these maps is that they are all a little different from each other, illustrating how closely each child was thinking about what specific information would be best to include and how to express those ideas visually. To introduce the activity, Lowell asked students to put themselves back in the activity itself. "Think about where you were when you were making your pattern. It's kind of the same context of reading closely, when you notice this is what happened, and this is what happened after. As a reader, as a thinker, and as a mathematician, you need to decide what needs to be recorded." Lowell also encouraged his students to slow down and really focus on the specific ideas and key information embedded within their math-and-dance patterns.

This idea of *slowing down* the mapping process and encouraging students to literally take it one step at a time is how the mapmaking becomes a way to reflect on one's work and an opportunity to communicate it in a new setting. At one point a student in Lowell's class was really struggling to remember and record her pattern while working seated at her desk. When she stood up, he told me, "she would physically do her pattern and then she'd look at the movement variables and write them down. Without her body involved, she was struggling big time, but when she stood up and she said, 'What am I doing? I am jumping right,' her body

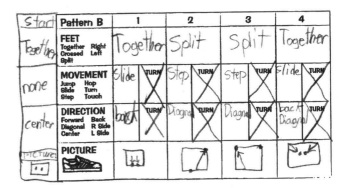

▶ **Figure 8.2** The pictures at the bottom on beats 2 and 3 make me think there's a turn on the third beat that didn't get recorded. This issue would likely come to light during a map exchange between teams of students.

▶ **Figure 8.3** This chart was intentionally designed to be structured but still open-ended, meaning that there will always be situations that arise that don't fit neatly into this recording system. Here, the student decided that he or she needed to record beat 0. I'm also interested in the use of the word split on beats 2 and 3. The step on beat 2 to the front corner could potentially be considered "on the diagonal," but only if the step on beat 3 landed in the opposite (back) corner instead of the front left corner. As it stands now, by the end of beat 3, both feet are split to the sides in the two front corners.

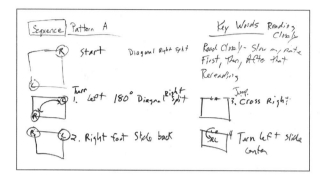

▶ **Figure 8.4**

communicated the information [back to her] so she was able to get it written down."

He continued, "I remember she was in a group that was dancing really quickly but not that accurately. She was able to slow herself down by saying to herself, 'OK, so this is my first move, what is that? How do I say that orally, what did I just do?'"

It's likely that most children will need to dance their pattern or see the pattern danced by their partner in order to record it. They can decide between them on the roles of mover and recorder as they collaborate on identifying the relevant properties.

Lowell modelled his own process of recording words and schematics on the board (see Figure 8.4) while he talked through the sequence of his own math-and-dance pattern. He focused students on the activities of reading and thinking closely about the steps, moving slowly, and rereading their work. See Figures 8.5 through 8.7 for some of the student work from that session.

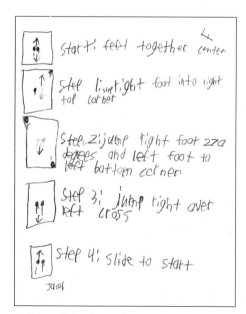

▶ **Figure 8.5** This map vertically sequences beat 0 through beat 4 using dots, arrows, and the language of the movement variables.

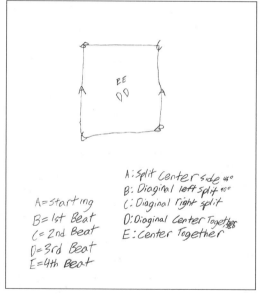

▶ **Figure 8.6** In this approach, each beat is designated by a letter (A through E), which is used as a way to indicate the order of the beats, the foot locations, and directions. However, no information is provided about the movements, which makes the pattern more difficult to reproduce.

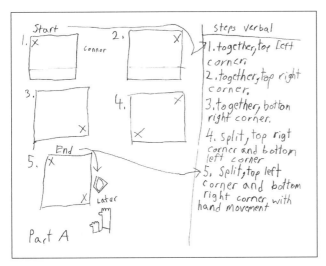

▶ **Figure 8.7** This map also seemingly ignores the movement aspect, but it is very detailed both verbally and spatially.

Defining Expectations for Contributing to the Problem-Solving Classroom Community

In addition to applying themselves to the creative mathematical problem solving, journaling, word study, and mapmaking, students are expected to be involved and engaged in the community of learning, including

- maintaining a positive working relationship with their partner;
- practicing and revising the creative work and maintaining a positive attitude when things get challenging;
- watching and responding to others' work with respect and interest; and
- working to understand the math in this new context.

Defining Expectations for a Final Product

Although students' growth and the process by which they make gains make up the main focus of the assessment process, if students make steady gains they will have something to show for it. By the end of the Math in Your Feet process, most students should

- have an eight-beat pattern they can remember and repeat (for certain students, creating and performing a four-beat pattern is success)

- be able to dance in unison with a partner at an agreed tempo, fast or slow

- have applied a transformation to their pattern at some point in the process, whether or not they've used it in their final eight-beat pattern

- have challenged themselves to create a pattern that includes elements that are potentially interesting to the viewer; for example, they have put some effort into making their pattern B "as different as possible" from their pattern A

Summing Up

Although these assessment ideas take a qualitative and descriptive approach to evaluating students' forward progress in the math-and-dance making, and are more focused on the process itself rather than the final skill set or product, we should still provide a clear set of expectations for student work and improvement. You communicate these expectations in context when you

- introduce the tools with which the children make their math-and-dance patterns,

- clearly lay out each new task,

- require positive participation during observation periods, and

- provide clear expectations during observation periods for positive audience behavior and feedback.

Overall, I am satisfied that learning is happening in my moving classroom when I observe things such as the following:

- A child who struggles with mathematics in other contexts devises a key problem-solving strategy and becomes an effective leader during a moving-scale math challenge.

- A child who was slow to warm up to the activity or has been reticent to show her math-and-dance work now willingly demonstrates in front of the class.

- A child who does not regularly join in on classroom discussions shares his thoughts while the class debriefs a moving-math challenge.

- A team that have been at odds for almost the entire process eventually work their way through the roadblocks to create a pattern that they can dance in unison.

- A team that moves easily from the start really challenges itself to make a second pattern that is *completely different* from its first pattern.

- A child who struggles with maintaining focus and composure in the classroom becomes a positive, patient, and supportive member of the math-and-dance-making community.

- The class as a whole self-regulates its activity in a busy, sometimes noisy classroom by relying on partners for ideas and problem solving, making positive decisions that lead students closer to the intended goal, and staying focused on their own work until it is time to reconvene as a class.

Overall, this approach to assessment is about expecting that the child will make something out of the experience to the best of her ability in a way that shows she wrestled with the ideas and challenges presented by the activity.

Extending and Connecting the Moving-Scale Math Experience

The moving-scale math and math-and-dance work are not panaceas for math education. Rather, they create a potent setting in which children dynamically engage in using, exploring, and expressing mathematical ideas. Using a math idea in multiple settings is what helps us understand it fully. To do this, students need opportunities to connect the math explored and experienced at moving scale to other mathematical settings and modes. This section lays out specific recommendations for making those connections. The suggestions for extending the moving-scale math work are embedded into the activity descriptions in Chapter 3, but many of the math read-alouds listed later in the chapter will be useful for both dance and nondance experiences.

Reflect and Connect: Math in Your Feet, Grades 3–6

This section is intended to give you an idea of the range of ways you can explore the ideas investigated and applied during the math-and-dance making and connect them to other contexts. You may also find other connections between the math-and-dance making and the math curriculum, language arts goals, and journals already in play in your classroom. Please use the following suggestions as starting places and inspiration for further connections. Note that suggestions for read-alouds appear in the next section.

Making Pattern A and Pattern B

- *Word study*: pattern, compare, congruent, similar, attribute, property
- *Sample journal prompts related to the math-and-dance-making activities*:

  Describe the pattern A you made with your partner. How did you know if you were dancing the same or not? (See Figure 8.8.)

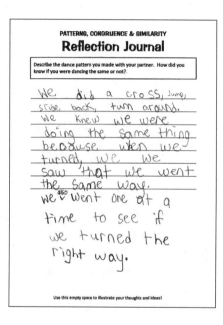

▶ **Figure 8.8** What's interesting here is that, initially, kids will use foot position words to write or talk about their patterns. In this case the student used movement words to describe her pattern and used the movement category to evaluate and describe sameness between her Patterns A and B.

You were asked to make your pattern B as different *as possible from your pattern A. What kinds of things did you and your partner have to consider to make sure pattern B was different? (See Figure 8.9.)*

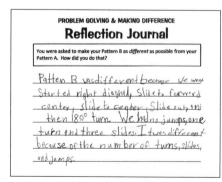

▶ **Figure 8.9** This description shows that the student is comparing the type of movements used in Pattern A and B to decide how they are different from each other. A next step might be to ask the student how s/he can be certain that the two patterns are as different as possible.

You can also give students a shorter, check-in reflection format. The prompts I have given include: *One thing I'll remember about my math-and-dance making today is . . .* ; *I still have questions about . . .* ; *What I'm finding hardest right now is . . .* ; and *What I liked best about today was. . . .* (See Figure 8.10.)

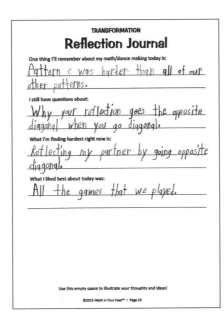

TRANSFORMATION

Reflection Journal

One thing I'll remember about my math/dance making today is:

Pattern c was harder than all of our other patterns.

I still have questions about:

Why your reflection goes the opposite diagonal when you go diagonal.

What I'm finding hardest right now is:

Reflecting my partner by going opposite diagonal.

What I liked best about today was:

All the games that we played.

Use this empty space to illustrate your thoughts and ideas!

©2015 Math in Your Feet™ • Page 19

▶ **Figure 8.10** This set of reflection prompts give you a good overview of how things are going and where the students' focus is at the moment. Here the student's response reflects on all three areas of the work: physical (making pattern C), mathematical (musing about the reflected patterns), and social (the reflection games).

Activities:

- Have students make a map (see "Making and Reading Maps (grades 3–6)" on page 149).

- Explore the idea of congruence using geometric forms, both on the page and handheld. When you can flip, slide, or turn a shape from any location so that it fits exactly on top of another shape, the two shapes are congruent. But what exactly needs to be the same? You may want to refer to your geometry unit for ideas about how to explore congruence using different handheld shapes as a way to compare and contrast it with the idea of sameness in the dancing. One class I worked with had explored congruence in both handheld and danced contexts, but some children had come to the conclusion that one team's dancing couldn't be considered the same because one teammate was much taller than the other. The opportunity to explore and discuss congruence in two different settings helped to expose the children's misconceptions and started a great conversation about defining and nondefining attributes and their role in determining congruence.

- Have students create an "attribute chain" with attribute blocks. This math tool is focused on finding commonalities between geometric shapes based on size, thickness, color, and shape. This is exactly the kind of work we do in Math in Your Feet as we evaluate the math-and-dance patterns for sameness, or congruence, between dancers in a team, or when teams are working to make their pattern B different from their pattern A.

- Add "Which One Doesn't Belong?" to your classroom math routines. This activity is like a visual puzzle with multiple right answers; the focus is on defining the ways three out of the four images are the same. You can explore similarity and congruence using the prompts at http://wodb.ca/shapes.html and explore number properties at http://wodb.ca/numbers.html (which also includes some useful contexts for using "WODB?" in general). For a comprehensive teachers guide and student edition go to http://www.stenhouse.com/wodb.

- Conduct a moving-scale math lesson, such as "Collaborative Rope Polygons" from Chapter 3.

- Play strategic tic-tac-toe, which emphasizes problem solving and spatial strategies. This game takes the traditional nine-cell version and creates a larger nine-cell grid with one smaller grid in each of the nine cells. Where you mark your X or O in one of the small grids determines where your opponent has to move next in the large grid, challenging players to harness their spatial reasoning for strategic thinking. For a more detailed explanation of how to play the game, see http://mathwithbaddrawings.com/2013/06/16/ultimate-tic-tac-toe/.

Executing Combination and Transformation

- *Word study:* sequence, combination

- *Sample journal prompts related to the math-and-dance-making activities:*

    What did you and your partner have to do to combine your patterns A and B?

*What changes did you have to make between beats 4 and 5
so that pattern C (eight beats) could be danced smoothly with
no pauses?*

Activities:

- Explore a variety of symmetries in a design context with
Symmetry Artist at the website Math Is Fun (www.mathsisfun
.com/geometry/symmetry-artist.html). The tool provides a large
inventory of options with which to create, save, and print designs.
Choose your attributes from the following categories: type of
symmetry (reflection or rotation); order and/or axis of symmetry;
and pen style, color, thickness, and transparency.

- Continue to include "Which One Doesn't Belong?" in your classroom math routines.

Reflect and Connect: Math in Your Feet, Grades K–2

Getting Started: Jumps and Steps in Center

- *Key vocabulary:* pattern, jump, step, center, middle, combine
- *Reflection 1* (for at least the first two sessions):

    What did you do today? Draw a picture of your dancing.

- *Visual reflection* (at least twice):

    What does your pattern look like? Draw a picture.

- *Reflection 2* (in conjunction with Reflections 1 and 2):

    What words can you use to describe your pattern?

Moving Out of Center: Expanding the Inventory of Directions

- *Key vocabulary:* pattern, front, back, side, corner, diagonal
- *Visual reflection or map* (at least twice):

    Where are your feet on each beat?

- *Reflection* (in conjunction with the visual reflection):

    What words did we use today?

Adding in a Split: Expanding the Inventory of Foot Positions

- *Key vocabulary:* split, front, back, side, corner, diagonal
- *Visual reflection or map:*

  Where are your feet on each beat?

- *Reflection* (in conjunction with the visual reflection):

  What words did we use today?

- *Reflection* (near the end of the process):

  What was your biggest challenge when making your dance pattern? Why?

Math Read-Alouds and Other Resources

The books in this section were chosen for their close connections to math topics and mathematical thinking embedded in the moving-scale math activities detailed in this book, their engaging narratives and illustrations, and their potential to spark conversations and inspire further exploration. And, because math learning can be very focused on specifics at times, I've also included selections that provide perspective on the larger "Why math?" questions. These are good resources for understanding and exploring a variety of mathematical patterns accessible to elementary students, as well as learning lovely bits of math history from ancient times through the present day, reminding all of us that while mathematics may appear to live inside our textbooks, it was actually created by curious humans over thousands of years in response to specific needs and questions.

Mathematical Relationships

Mathematical relationships are defined through the activity of making comparisons, something we do a lot of in the math-and-dance making. The following suggestions provide ample opportunity to see how this might work in a variety of other contexts. I chose these books because of their evocative storytelling and illustrations, which, like all good stories, can lead you and your class directly into the wonderful world of having conversations about mathematical ideas. You might recognize some of these specifically as math related, while others are less obvious, but each entry includes an overview of the kind of math to look for as you read. These books connect to both the Math in Your Feet work and many of the moving-scale activities in Chapter 3.

Primary Grades

Caps for Sale: A Tale of a Peddler, Some Monkeys and Their Monkey Business, by Esphyr Slobodkina (New York: W. R. Scott, 1947)

Math: categories, positional language, sequential ordering and language, patterning

Caps for Sale is a classic children's book chock-full of math! Are the caps in the same order at the end of the story as they were at the beginning?

Beep, Beep, Vroom, Vroom, by Stuart Murphy (New York: Harper Collins, 2000)

Math: sequence, combination, attributes, patterning

As Molly plays with her big brother's toy cars, she inadvertently puts them into disorder. Can she put the cars back in the right order before her brother returns?

What's Next Nina? by Sue Kassirer (New York: Kane Press, 2001)

Math: sequential ordering and language, combination, attributes, patterning

A borrowed string of beads breaks unexpectedly and Nina has to hurry to remember the original order of the beading design. Diversity is represented in the illustrations.

Hannah's Collections, by Marthe Jocelyn (New York: Dutton, 2001)

Math: sorting, classifying, attributes, visual patterns and groupings, ordering, number combinations, problem solving

A collection is a group of things that share one or more common attribute. This book is full of images to look at and notice and wonder about and, maybe, inspire your students to create, share, and explain their own collections! What do the objects in the collection have in common? What differences do you see?

Primary and Intermediate

Five Creatures, by Emily Jenkins (New York : Frances Foster Books, 2001)

Math: relationships, attributes, comparisons, similarities, differences

"Five creatures live in our house. Three humans, and two cats. Three short, and two tall. Four grownups, and one child (that's me!)." This is an absolutely charming book that illustrates all the ways a family of five are similar and different. Some of these comparisons are easy to figure out; others require some close looking. Either way, you'll be delighted by what you find.

How to Make an Apple Pie and See the World, by Marjorie Priceman (New York: Alfred A. Knopf, 1994)

Math: sequencing, algorithm

Both our math-and-dance patterns and an apple pie are created with a certain logical ordering, and both are made from an inventory of things with which to create a new whole (math-and-dance pattern unit or pie). The illustrations in this book, appropriate for grades K–3, show a young girl visiting various agrarian locations around the world to pick up different ingredients for her pie.

Somewhere in the World Right Now, by Stacy Schuett (New York: Knopf, 1995)

Math: sameness, similarity, difference, attributes

This book is ostensibly about geography, but I also see a lot of math. The premise of the story is that when one child is sleeping, another is just waking up in a different part of the world. The words and illustrations highlight our similarities and differences as humans as we go about our days, no matter where we are located on the map.

Mathematical Patterns

Students often leave elementary school understanding patterns as things that repeat when in fact there are a plethora of rich and diverse mathematical patterns. The following books will help students experience the many different patterns we can find and use in math.

All Grades

Patterns, What Are They? by William Shimek (Minneapolis: Lerner Publications Co., 1969)

Math: understanding different kinds of patterns

This book provides examples of the many different kinds of patterns we can find around us, including patterns that help us create or predict things, patterns of odd and even numbers, and square and cubed numbers. This book was published in 1969 but there are PDF copies available for download online.

***Patterns*, by David Kirkby (Crystal Lake, IL: Rigby Interactive Library, 1996)**

Math: number, shape, space, position, graphs, rotations, tilings, tessellations, spirals, mathematical stars, ordering, combination, codes, number patterns, multiplication patterns, number shapes, curves and straight lines

Another look at the big picture of what mathematical patterns look like and can do. Each section includes activity suggestions.

***The King's Chessboard*, by David Birch (New York: Puffin Books, 1988)**

Math: number patterns, doubling

The king wishes to reward an advisor, who in return refuses payment. The king presses for an answer and the advisor acquiesces by asking to be paid in rice, starting with one grain and doubling from there, illustrating how quickly the pattern of doubling can get out of hand. (This book also ties well to the "Proving Center" activity, on page 49.)

***Anno's Mysterious Multiplying Jar*, by Masaichiro Anno and Mitsumasa Anno (New York: Philomel Books, 1983)**

Math: multiplication, number patterns, ordering, combinations, factorials

This book is a gorgeously illustrated story "about numbers and how they can expand almost without limit . . . [giving] readers an idea of the remarkable order that underlies our universe, and a sense of the mystery, wonder, and excitement that can be experienced through mathematics" (Anno and Anno 1983).

Number and Shape

These books relate especially to the "Proving Center" and "Scaling Up" activities from Chapter 3.

Primary Grades

***Equal Shmequal*, by Virginia Kroll (Watertown, MA: Charlesbridge, 2005)**

Math: equal, half, fair sharing, attributes, groups, balance, measurement, symmetry, number, sorting, classifying

This is an engaging, action-packed tale about all the different ways we can think about and use *equal*. Children will enjoy and learn from the different ways the animal characters work together to figure out what *equal* really means. Teachers will enjoy having such a memorable tale to use as a benchmark experience for this multifaceted idea.

Not Enough Room! by Joanne Rocklin (New York: Scholastic, 1998)

Math: half, equal shares, problem solving, geometry

There's a baby on the way and two sisters discover this means they will need to share a room. But how to do it fairly? As the story progresses, the sisters explore different ways to partition their room in half. The end of the book includes activities for retelling the story and exploring other ways to figure out what "half of a rectangle" can look like. Includes images of diverse learners.

The Lion's Share, by Matthew McElligott (New York: Walker Publishing Company, 2009)

Math: halves, doubles, fair sharing, fractions, division, multiplication

The Lion King invites his subjects to dinner and asks his guests to share his cake. The greedy, ill-mannered guests all want a piece, of course. When it becomes clear that halving the cake over and over does not allow everyone to have the same amount, the guests go out of their way to top each other in providing replacement cakes. Unfortunately, when you double a number repeatedly, things get out of hand quite quickly!

Round Is a Mooncake, by Roseanne Thong (San Francisco: Chronicle Books, 2000)

Math: shapes in everyday life, geometry

Through gentle, rhyming text and lovely illustrations, readers follow a young Chinese girl as she travels through her urban neighborhood finding shapes. Best of all, the shapes she finds have personal meaning to her life and experience.

Primary and Intermediate

Most of these books relate to the Math in Your Feet work and the "Collaborative Rope Polygons" activity in Chapter 3.

***Ten Times Better*, by Richard Michelson (New York: Marshall Cavendish, 2000)**

Math: multiplication, scale, relational language (*farther*, *taller*, *stronger*, etc.)

The story itself is simple and charming but the back of the book holds amazing information from which physical body-based challenges can be created. The author asks readers to consider the attributes of twenty or so animals and asks them to think about how they might fare in comparison. Scale can be an elusive concept, but ten times bigger, longer, faster, smaller, and so on is a large enough amount to make an impact, psychologically speaking, on kids who know intuitively that they are small creatures in an adult-sized world. See http://mathinyourfeet.blogspot.com/2013/01/ten-times-better-longer-faster-farther.html for a related activity.

***The Greedy Triangle*, by Marilyn Burns (New York: Scholastic, 1994)**

Math: polygons, polygon properties, sides, angles

A dissatisfied triangle visits a shape-shifter, asking again and again for "one more side and one more angle." From triangle to decagon and beyond, readers get a chance to examine the properties and attributes of various polygons and the effect of having too many sides. (This book relates to the "Collaborative Rope Polygons" and "Scaling Up" activities in Chapter 3 and the Math in Your Feet work as well.)

***Chasing Vermeer*, by Blue *Balliett* (New York: Scholastic, 2004)**

Math: pentominoes, ciphers, codes, rectangles, geometry, math practices and problem solving

This incredibly engaging novel centers on an art scandal and mystery, which is ultimately solved by two persistent twelve-year-olds. An introduction to the mathematics of pentominoes and how they relate to the code in the book is provided, including some encouraging words about the nature of mathematical problem solving.

***The Fly on the Ceiling: A Math Reader*, by Julie Glass (New York: Random House, 1998)**

Math: mapping, grids, coordinate graphing, organizing information

This classic fictional biography of René Descartes, who popularized the Cartesian coordinate system, hilariously illustrates the need for mathematical tools and systems to help us organize information.

***What's Your Angle, Pythagoras?* by Julie Ellis (Watertown: Charlesbridge, 2004)**

> *Math:* angles, right angles, square numbers, problem solving and math practices, math history

> In this book, young Pythagoras is an enthusiastic and curious boy who investigates and ultimately solves some real-life issues for his father. The story and the mathematics blend well in this engaging story.

***Spaghetti and Meatballs for All!* by Marilyn Burns (New York: Scholastic, 1997)**

> *Math:* combinations, square units, polygons, area, perimeter, math practices

> This funny and delightful book tells the tale of finding just the right seating arrangement for a large family dinner. In the back of the book there are some notes to teachers as well as activity suggestions to help children makes sense of the mathematics in the story.

***Toads and Tessellations,* by Sharon Morrisette (Watertown: Charlesbridge, 2012)**

> *Math:* polygons, tessellations, transformation, symmetry, math practices and problem solving, math history

> How can you make twelve pairs of shoes out of one piece of leather? This story mixes magic and mathematics and some playful problem solving. A glossary of math terms and a note about the math are provided at the back of the book. If you read it a second time, students can look for over twenty-five different tessellations hidden in the illustrations throughout the book.

The Mathematical Big Picture

Here are a few books that can provide you and your students some perspective and insight into the big picture of why and how mathematics came to be and how it is used in the world in both play and work.

Grades 2–6

The Great Number Rumble: A Story of Math in Surprising Places, by Cora Lee and Gilian O'Reilly (Ontario: Annick Press Ltd., 2007)

The Great Number Rumble, best suited to students in grades 3–6, extends an enthusiastic, positively pitched hand out to everyone who thinks math has no relevance in his or her life. The narrative revolves around Sam, a self-proclaimed "math-nik," as he shows his entire school how math is useful in modern-day pursuits. From bike riding to CGI effects to music making, this engaging narrative helps readers see how the math in their textbooks is present in their everyday interests and activities. There are also sidebars that introduce interesting, often gory, tidbits of math history.

The History of Counting, by Denise Schmandt-Besserat (New York: William Morrow *and* Company Inc., 1999)

Even if math is not our favorite subject, we still can still marvel at what it would be like to live in a world without numbers or that there are systems of counting that are executed by pointing to different parts of our body. This gorgeous and softly illustrated book should be taken in slowly as children and adults alike grasp the accomplishment of how humans went from managing without numbers all the way to the invention of abstract numbers as tools for counting and computing.

G Is for Googol: A Math Alphabet Book, by David M. Schwartz (New York: Random House, 1998)

This is an amazing and beautiful book with mathematical entries for each letter of the alphabet. These entries provide an enthusiastic and interesting overview of tons of interesting math ideas. Many of these entries offer inspiration for mini-activities in your own classroom. Read it one or two entries at a time, or leave it out for kids to ponder over.

The Cat in Numberland, by Ivar Ekeland (Chicago: Cricket Books, 2006)

This book, best for grades 3–6, tells a unique story of numbers living and playing in the Hotel Infinity in which readers learn many interesting things about the weird ways that infinity behaves. The story is not really about the cat, but she does have some useful questions.

Final Thoughts

Considering and understanding the whole moving body as a source of cognition and learning in the elementary classroom is still a fairly new effort, with the exception of school-based creative dance programs, which are, honestly, few and far between. Our preschool colleagues have been implementing meaningful whole-body-based education since Friedrich Froebel "invented" kindergarten in the early 1800s. But, much less is known about how and why to blend mathematical content—not math as memorization—into meaningful, developmentally appropriate experiences for children beyond the preschool years. My hope is that the activities in this book instigate further conversation, experimentation, critique, and collaboration, leading to continuing improvements and innovations in pedagogy and approach in moving-scale math learning in elementary schools.

Now it's time for you to get started! As you take your first steps, please consider reaching out for support from other educators in your school community and online. You can check in at the *Math on the Move* blog for discussions and new resources at:

https://mathonthemovebook.com

Also, remember to access our video and resoures (see directions on pages xvii and xix). Or you can meet me and others doing this work on Twitter (I'm at @mathinyourfeet). While you're there, check in on the #movingmath and #miyfeet hashtags from time to time to pose questions or participate in organized chats. You can also join the *Math on the Move[Book]* Facebook book group (www.facebook.com/groups/MathOnTheMove/), a place for conversation, question asking, and obtaining support from other educators who, like you, are helping their students harness their endless natural energy and body knowledge for mathematical sense making.

Appendix

Videos

Here are some lively examples of foot-based percussive dance plus a couple more moving-math videos to inspire you and your students.

- High-energy Appalachian clogging and flatfooting, with just the feet in the frame: https://youtu.be/337_Vzqn91Y.

- Irish fiddle music and step dance from Liz Carrol and Nic Gareiss: https://youtu.be/ph0mdXxDA7Y.

- Dance forms of Mexico's son huasteco style: https://youtu.be/W7akhGd9ejQ. The dancer, Artemio Posadas, does a little demonstration in the middle of the video that shows the softer sounds very clearly.

- The Nicholas Brothers, tap dance legends, in a classic scene from the movie *Stormy Weather*: https://youtu.be/fNKRm6H-qOU. Athletic, musical, and great at dancing in small spaces!

- Irish sean-nós (old style) step dancers: https://youtu.be/-DB7naPkzKg. See what you think in terms of similarities and differences between the Mexican and Irish percussive dance styles.

- In this clip from the movie *Duck Soup*, the Marx Brothers get mathematically goofy: https://youtu.be/rdQ9jh5GvQ8. Who's the reflection here, do you think?

- Micro origami unfolds in water: https://youtu.be/n51Vi3rv_kA. Mesmerizing and mathematical.

Music Suggestions

Here are some music suggestions to get you started. These three tracks will give you an idea of a not-too-fast, not-too-slow tempo (speed) for this kind of dancing, and all are available on iTunes. Your building's music specialist may have music to pull from as well. Tempo and a strong, steady pulse are the most important factors in choosing music for the dancing.

- "Ocean," by the Heartbeats Rhythm Quartet (from the album *Spinning World*)
- "The Flowing Bowl" and "Níl Na Lá," by Solas (from the album *Solas*)

References

Alibali, Martha W., and Mitchell J. Nathan. 2012. "Embodiment in Mathematics Teaching and Learning: Evidence from Learners' and Teachers' Gesture." *The Journal of the Learning Sciences* 21 (2): 247–86.

Anno, Masaichiro, and Mitsumasa Anno. 1983. *Anno's Mysterious Multiplying Jar.* New York: Philomel Books.

Ball, Deborah Loewenberg. 1990. *With an Eye on the Mathematical Horizon: Dilemmas of Teaching Elementary School Mathematics.* East Lansing, MI: Michigan State University.

———. 1992. "Magical Hopes: Manipulatives and the Reform of Math Education." *American Educator* 16 (2): 14–18, 46–47.

Baratta-Lorton, Mary. 1995. *Mathematics Their Way: An Activity-Centered Mathematics Program for Early Childhood Education.* 20th anniv. ed. Parsippany, NJ: Addison-Wesley.

Beacon Educator. n.d. "Frayer Model." Reading Educator. www.readingeducator.com/strategies/frayer.htm. Retrieved March 15, 2016.

Caspersz, Shereese Halley. n.d. "Exploring Symmetry Through Dance" (Video). www.teachingchannel.org/videos/teaching-symmetry-with-dance.

Committee on Support for Thinking Spatially: The Incorporation of Geographic Information Science Across the K–12 Curriculum, Geographic Science Committee, Board on Earth Sciences and Resources, Division on Earth and Life Studies, and the National Research Council. 2006. *Learning to Think Spatially: GIS as a Support System in the K–12 Curriculum.* Washington, DC: National Academies Press.

Danielson, Christopher. 2012. "One Is One . . . or Is It?" (TED-Ed video). Published May 21. https://youtu.be/EtclcWGG7WQ.

———. 2013. Personal communication.

DetroitYouthVideos. 2013. "El Arte: 2nd Grade Dance/Math Lesson." (Video). June 24. http://youtu.be/MWMwWqOeluk.

Dewey, John. 1938. *Experience and Education* New York: Macmillan: Kappa Delta Pi.

Flanagan, Nancy. 2013. "STEAM-Roller." *Teacher in a Strange Land* (blog), October 31. http://blogs.edweek.org/teachers/teacher_in_a_strange_land/2013/10/steam-roller.html.

Hall, Rogers, Jasmine Y. Ma, and Ricardo Nemirovsky. 2015. "Re-scaling Bodies in/as Representational Instruments in GPS Drawing." In *Learning Technologies and the Body: Integration and Implementation in Formal and Informal Learning Environments*, edited by Victor R. Lee, 112–31. New York: Routledge.

Hall, Rogers, and Ricardo Nemirovsky. 2011. "Histories of Modal Engagements with Mathematical Concepts: A Theory Memo." Tangible Math. August 22. www.sci.sdsu.edu/tlcm/all-articles/Histories_of_modal_engagement_with_mathematical_concepts.pdf.

Hines, Gregory, host. 1989. "Gregory Hines: Tap Dance in America." *Great Performances*. Don Mischer Productions/KQED.

Martinez, Sylvia Libow, and Gary Stager. 2013. *Invent to Learn: Making, Tinkering, and Engineering in the Classroom*. Torrance, CA: Constructing Modern Knowledge.

Moses, Robert P., and Charles E. Cobb, Jr. 2002. *Radical Equations: Civil Rights from Mississippi to the Algebra Project*. Boston: Beacon.

National Governors Association (NGA) Center for Best Practices and Council of Chief State School Officers (CCSSO). 2010. *Common Core State Standards for Mathematics*. Washington, DC: NGA Center for Best Practices and CCSSO. www.corestandards.org/assets/CCSSI_Math%20Standards.pdf.

Papert, Seymour. 1993. *Mindstorms: Children, Computers, and Powerful Ideas*. 2d ed. New York: Basic Books.

Picciotto, Henri. n.d. "For a Tool-Rich Pedagogy." Henri Picciotto's Math Education Page. www.mathedpage.org/tools/tools.html. Retrieved March 14, 2016.

Queen's Printer for Ontario. 2014. *Paying Attention to Spatial Reasoning*. Toronto: Ontario Ministry of Education. www.edu.gov.on.ca/eng/literacynumeracy/LNSPayingAttention.pdf.

Ray, Max. 2013. *Powerful Problem Solving: Activities for Sense Making with the Mathematical Practices*. Portsmouth, NH: Heinemann.

Ruggery, Jenni. 2012. "Math Dance." (Video). November 29. www.youtube.com/watch?v=uSd6TqQ6oKY.

Sarama, Julie, and Douglas Clements. 2009. *Early Childhood Mathematics Education Research: Learning Trajectories for Young Children*. New York: Routledge.

Sfard, Anna. 1991. "On the Dual Nature of Mathematical Conceptions: Reflections on Processes and Objects as Different Sides of the Same Coin." *Educational Studies in Mathematics* 22 (1): 1–36.

Smith, Carmen Petrick, Barbara King, and Jennifer Hoyte. 2014. "Learning Angles Through Movement: Critical Actions for Developing Understanding in an Embodied Activity." *The Journal of Mathematical Behavior* 36 (December): 95–108.

Smith, Linda, and Michael Gasser. 2005. "The Development of Embodied Cognition: Six Lessons from Babies." *Artificial Life* 11 (1–2): 13–29.